A Book of Days for Lent

Feast and Fast

Fast from
    Discontent,
    Anger,
    Bitterness,
    Self-concern,
    Discouragement,
    Laziness,
    Suspicion,
    Guilt,
    Hopelessness and fear.

Feast on
    Gratitude,
    Patience,
    Generosity,
    Commitment,
    Compassion for others,
    Trust,
    Forgiveness,
    Hope and wonder,
    Truth and the mercy of God.

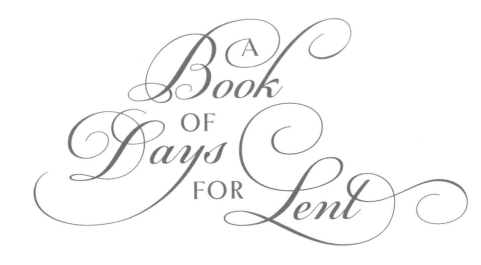

A Book OF Days FOR Lent

Daily Reflections
for the Season of Lent

Seedbed

SEEDBED PUBLISHING
Franklin, Tennessee
Seedbed.com

Contents

Acknowledgments

Rest and be thankful.
—William Wordsworth

The season of Lent is often coupled with the acts of resting, pausing, and remembering so that one can recognize and express gratitude and appreciation for people, works, sacrifices, and answered prayers. As we begin this journey to the cross of our Savior, we pause to acknowledge and thank some of the many individuals who made this project possible.

We first want to acknowledge the creative collaboration and leadership of Murdock's 2015 and 2016 interns, Shawna Gordon and Kehlay Dunah.

Shawna's thoughtful consideration of "the journey to the cross" framed the mission of each meditation. We are thankful for her creative framing and organization of the book. She skillfully passed the project to create a seamless transition to Kehlay, who managed the project to completion. Both women dedicated much time and energy in the entire process of creating this meditation book.

We also want to acknowledge Stefanie Narhi, the extraordinary executive assistant at the M. J. Murdock Trust. We thank Stefanie for her organization and guidance through the entirety of this project. She supported Shawna and Kehlay, guiding them as leaders and managers, proofreading documents, and helping see this book to completion.

Our friends at Seedbed Publishing were also wonderful partners throughout the entire journey of bringing this book together. We especially thank Andrew Miller and J. D. Walt, along with Nick Perreault, Maren Kurek, Renee Chavez, and Holly Jones for their meticulous work behind the scenes editing, transforming Word documents into brilliant works, and bringing this book to life. It is always a pleasure working with such dedicated and talented individuals who help others make dreams become reality.

I, Steve, would like to give thanks for my parents and parents-in-law: Wilford and Marian Moore and Ken and Jean Kelly; for my children: Maegan, Mollie, Madison, and his wife, Chandi, who have been the source of such joy, insight, and love, and are great gifts of grace and wonder from God; and last and especially, for my incredibly gifted, patient, and loving wife, Thanne, who is an agent of grace, goodness, and love.

I, Rick, acknowledge how slowly I have been able to comprehend the nature and depth of the "we" from which I come, and because of which I can proceed with confidence into the closing acts of my life. I acknowledge that I come from a family of Christian faith in its Catholic expression, and have had forty-two years of my life in the complex grace that is the Society of Jesus (the Jesuits). In particular, and in relation to this book, I want to thank my Jesuit provincial, Scott Santarosa, S. J. and my fellow Jesuits in Oregon. I am especially thankful for the board of the Faber Institute, Greg Specht, Janeen McAninch, Pat Golding, Pietro Ferrari, Bruce Bolton, and Craig Boly, S. J. Their belief in me and support is amazing and providential. I also am so thankful for my Faber colleague, Mary Carter Edmonds.

To our contributors we extend the utmost gratitude. It is by their dedication, creative excellence, generosity, and wisdom that this book was crafted. The meditations found in this book reflect the time they, too, spent journeying to the cross and living resurrection and are an invitation for us all to do the same. These contributing writers represent organizations, institutions, partners, friends, and colleagues that make up a vibrant fabric of amazing leaders.

Last, but certainly not least, we recognize and express gratitude to Lyn and Karin Swanson, John and Sarah Castles, and Jeff and Sandy Grubb for their love, guidance, encouragement, and support. Lyn, John, and Jeff serve on the Board of Trustees for the M. J. Murdock Charitable Trust, and seek to fulfill the mission "to nurture and enrich the spiritual, educational, cultural, and social life of individuals, families, and communities." They serve in this role with grace, wisdom, faithfulness, and steadfastness. And for our colleagues and friends with whom we have the privilege to work at the M. J. Murdock Charitable Trust: they are patient, exceedingly gifted, and dedicated to flourishing and practicing resurrection in all that they do. Together we seek to offer common grace for the common good.

For all others, forgive our forgetfulness and failure to acknowledge your grace and encouragement in our lives. We are surrounded by a great cloud of witnesses. Finally, to the MOWPDX/OHM BOYZ—you rock!

—Steve and Rick

Introduction

The season of Lent is one for preparation and repentance, laying down oneself to embrace the Savior who laid down himself for us. It is paradoxically both beautiful and painful, intentionally journeying toward the cross. That is exactly what the purpose of this Lenten devotional is: a journey toward the cross. A journey that doesn't simply begin in the New Testament but in Genesis, through Exodus and the laws of Leviticus, through the Kings and the Prophets, and through the Wisdom Literature of Scripture. It would be a disservice to include only New Testament literature, as Christ's death on the cross would make sense only with a holistic view of why he lived and died for us.

Within this journey thematically are postures each week that Jesus took on through his own life. Each week's writer encourages us to intentionally take on the posture as well, allowing us to immerse ourselves in the words, life, death, and resurrection of Jesus Christ. It is our hope that as each week highlights a different posture, we are able to walk through the season of Lent to the celebration of Easter and the days of resurrected life! We pray these writings encourage a conscious mind-set of what it means to journey toward the cross, and then to the empty tomb.

First Week of Lent

HUMILITY

Christ Washing the Apostles' Feet
by Dirck van Baburen (1594–1624)

This Dutch painter of Utrecht, who lived only to twenty-nine years old, was deeply impacted by the artistic innovations of the widely influential Caravaggio of Italy (1571–1610). He went at the age of sixteen to Italy to study with the Italian master painters, learning his craft in their workshops over the course of nine years, before returning to Utrecht.[1]

To notice: (1) The man at front and left has crossed his left leg over his right knee, which allows us to see that the feet that we are talking about—the ones that Jesus knelt to wash—were actually dirty! True acts of godliness and right religion do not overlook the actual, practical help offered others when we notice that they need help washing up. (2) This act of divine humility and human thoughtfulness by Jesus creates a division in the room. Half of them are attending in one direction; Jesus and the others are attending in the other direction. Why does Jesus' humility appear to split the group, and even cause arguments in both groups to break out? (3) Observe each of the hands that van Baburen paints: the specific expressiveness of each, and especially the hands of Jesus on Peter's leg and foot and those of Peter—one over his heart; one so tenderly on Jesus' left elbow.

bpk, Berlin/Gemäeldegalerie/ Jörg P. Anders/Art Resource, NY

First Sunday of Lent

STEVE MOORE

❖

LUKE 4:16–22 • ROMANS 12:1–3

Don't cherish exaggerated ideas of yourself or your importance, but try to have a sane estimate of your capabilities by the light of the faith that God has given to you all.
Romans 12:3 (PHILLIPS)

For Reluctant Travelers

What a strange place to begin the Lenten journey: with humility. I must confess that every time I begin the journey to Easter, I groan a bit. I think to myself: *What can I give up that will cause little disruption or sense of loss?* I continue to build the case for my thinking, *How can I avoid the things that might disrupt or derail my busy daily life? I have too many things going on to rethink, reorder, or reorganize my life! Could we just get to Easter and the Hallelujah Chorus please?*

Then humility the size of a mustard seed gets planted in my heart and I remember why this Lenten journey is a gift that believers from the earliest days of the church began to encourage and seek. They encouraged, taught, and practiced this spiritual exercise because they too needed a season to recalibrate to living and practicing resurrection as a daily means of grace.

I love the painting we enjoyed this week, *Christ Washing the Apostles' Feet*. It captures how so many of us feel as we begin this journey and as we consider humility. In the painting there are expressions of surprise, protest, denial, argument, and confusion. The disciples, like us, keep getting surprised by Jesus. He thinks, acts, speaks, and does everything so . . . differently. At first it seems he is so out of step with everything around him. He seems so out of rhythm with the world of his day (as well as the days in which you and I live!). He is badly out of step, and maybe off key. What in the world is he thinking; where is he coming from?

But then we begin to hear, ever so lightly, the rhythm and music that guides his life. We hear the words and they refresh our heart and soul. We begin to realize it is not he who is out of rhythm, it is us. The rhythm of the world in which he lived (like our world) is in fact discordant, off key, sometimes sung with despair, often full of half-truths.

Ann Weems is a mother, writer, and thinker. After losing her son and sinking into what felt like drowning darkness, she managed to hear and write these words:

> In the godforsaken, obscene quicksand of life,
> there is a deafening alleluia
> rising from the souls of those who weep,
> and of those who weep with those who weep.
> If you watch, you will see
> the hand of God
> putting the stars back in their skies
> one by one.[2]

"A deafening alleluia." I like that. I need that.

Jim Dodson tells the story of a conversation he had with a friend as he was about to begin the journey of Lent. He was, like me, complaining and dragging his feet a bit. His friend surprised him with this thought, "Lent, I sometimes think, is when we take darkness of our failed hopes and schemes to an empty tomb, only to discover that something has indeed changed, a candle lit, and something risen. Despite our worst fears, we're more alive than ever, and now we have the chance to make a better world."[3]

I don't know where you find yourself as you begin this journey of Lent. It may be that your life is rocking along just fine. It may be that you are coming out of a season of questioning and doubt. It may be that you find yourself out of gas, depleted from a season of challenges and difficult work. It may be you are in the midst of a fruitful and joyous time of life. In whatever place you find yourself, you are invited to intentionally, deliberately, and humbly open yourself to the forty-day journey ahead. Christ will come along with us, speaking to the realities of our lives in ways that will bring life, shed light, and refresh our journey. He will no doubt surprise us . . . again.

Lord we come to you as sometimes reluctant, sometimes eager, travelers. Be patient with our impatience. Forgive our flimsy confidence in our own strength and sense of self-satisfaction. Meet us in these days and create in us a clean heart where your grace may do its work.

Steve and his wife, Thanne, have four adult children, Madison and Chandi, Maegan and Mollie. Steve works at the M. J. Murdock Charitable Trust.

First Monday of Lent

BRIAN DOYLE

❈

GENESIS 2:1–9 • LUKE 19:28–40

. . . The LORD God made the earth and the heavens, And every plant of the field before it was in the earth, and every herb of the field before it grew . . . But there went up a mist from the earth, and watered the whole face of the ground. And the LORD God formed man of the dust of the ground . . .
Genesis 2:4–7 (KJV)

This Wild and Precious Life

First lesson, cousins: remember that we are made of the dust of the earth, of the stuff of the stars, and all pose and pomp and arrogance and attitude are as grains of sand against the wind, soon to be scattered. *So what is it you will do with your one wild and precious life,* as the great poet Mary Oliver asks? As your shaggy teammate in this vale of tears and laughter, I might suggest this: that we remember humility is where real wisdom lives; that tenderness and witness and reverence are the bones of all religions and all true greatness; that holding hands against the dark and reaching for others' hands when they are lost and reaching to help with the loads others stumble under is true greatness; that the pinnacles of finance and power and celebrity are the smallest of feats; that imagination and humor and mercy are the tools which may yet change the world, and send violence and greed wailing and gnashing into oblivion; that we are graced and blessed to draw breath, to be here on earth with our living and sentient companions, the plants, and animals, in a world teeming with beauty and love.

We are each a shard of light. The more we join shard to shard, the greater the light; and someday, somehow, evil will wither and fade. That will be a great day, a holy day, a wonderful day. I pray our children's children see it dawn.

> *Dear Coherent Mercy, as the great Barry Lopez*
> *calls The Love; dear "Chief Musician," as the*
> *Psalms have it, give us the strength to bring our*
> *gifts like weapons against the dark. Please.*

Brian Doyle is the editor of *Portland Magazine* at the University of Portland, and the author of many books, notably the novel *Mink River* and the essay collection *Children & Other Wild Animals*.

First Tuesday of Lent

STEPHEN NEWBY

❖

ROMANS 5:12–16 • MATHEW 8:14–17

But the free gift is not like the trespass. For if many died through one man's trespass, much more have the grace of God and the free gift in the grace of that one man Jesus Christ abounded for many.
Romans 5:15 (RSV)

Embracing Grace for the Journey

A young man was asked to lead a short prayer for a program where he attended school. An hour before the event, a friend asked if he was nervous. Having read prayers many times before, he boldly responded: "No. I've done this before." When the time came for him to recite the prayer, he walked carefully and confidently to the podium. Clearing his throat, he began to read. Suddenly, his eyes were unfocused on the page. Unable to be fully present within the prayer, he began reading words erroneously, ruining the rhythm of the text, and distorting the prayer altogether. He felt undone. Silence ensued. Leaving the podium, he felt humiliated and humbled by his failure to deliver what was asked of him.

Do you feel as if you have failed God lately? Have you ever felt embarrassed to pray to God? Are you able to be fully present with God in your prayers? Are your spiritual eyes unfocused? In this season of Lent, as silence ensues upon our reflections, we are humbled by God's verdict of acquittal upon our lives. We all make mistakes. Romans 5:15b states: "the free gift in the grace of that one man Jesus Christ abounded for many" (RSV). Christ gives to us the grace so as to keep the rhythms of our petitions synced with God's breath of life. Today, let's clear our minds of every burden that so easily besets us, seeking the wise Creator's gift to us with a humble boldness.

Dear Gracious Sovereign Lord,
Although at times we fail you, we thank you for
your great gift of grace, which fully comes to us in
our time of need. We come to you with a humble
boldness, waiting for the day of our resurrection. We
believe we will be healed and raised from all disease,
pain, and corruption. Bring healing to our land, to
our spiritual legacies, and to our languished tongues.
Lord Jesus Christ, even in our failures, forgive us and
help us to respond to your gift of grace with a humble
boldness, serving humanity and your will.
In the name of the Father, Son, and Holy Spirit.
Amen.

Composer, author, and worship leader, Stephen Newby is director of the Center for Worship and associate professor of Music at Seattle Pacific University. He also serves as pastor of Worship Arts at Antioch Bible Church in Kirkland, Washington. He, his wife, Stephanie, and their son, Silas, live in Bothell, Washington.

Ash Wednesday

ALAN HAMILTON

❖

PSALM 79 • JOHN 15:1–6

Do not hold against us the sins of past generations; may your mercy come quickly to meet us, for we are in desperate need. Help us, God our Savior, for the glory of your name; deliver us and forgive our sins for your name's sake.

Psalm 79:8–9 (NIV)

Let It Find You

Humility is an elusive quality. The minute you work your hardest to obtain it, you become proud. The very pursuit disqualifies you at the outset. How can you grasp it? You don't. You do not find humility, it finds you. And, it almost certainly enters through the back door of failure and hardship. Not an easy path. But the view from there is easily the best you will ever find. It is unobstructed by self. No selfies or selfishness or self-interest there. Just him. And when you see him, it becomes the most beautiful thing you will ever know.

Where were you when humility entered your life? Where did life take on rich meaning? Before you answer, recognize that your answer cannot possibly include your own effort and accomplishment, even in the form of right living and excellent choices. Humility is found when you see yourself as you really are. All the mess, in clear view. If you can personally and specifically know why Jesus died for you, you stand a chance of really living. There is no way to get there without true and complete dependence. It is truly all about him. Less of you is more of him. What's the path to that life? Simple. Get out of the way! Recognize that everything you have is from God. If you fail to feel that, ask him to help you. Pain and difficulty may follow, but a view (even a glimpse) of his goodness will forever change you.

Father, give us the will to see ourselves as we really are, and in that darkness to know you bring light and hope and forgiveness. May your mercy come quickly to meet us, for we are in desperate need.

Alan Hamilton is the executive director of Clark County Food Bank, making sure that hungry kids and families get fed and cared for. His path to humility is filled with failure and grief, mercy and grace.

First Thursday of Lent

ATUL TANDON

❋

ISAIAH 42 • JOHN 1:1–5

"I am the Lord, I have called you in righteousness,
I have taken you by the hand and kept you;
I have given you as a covenant to the people, a light to the nations."
Isaiah 42:6 (RSV)

Pride's Remedy

This daily journey in the season of Lent brings to mind the steep chasm between a holy, loving God and the prideful humanity he calls his own. What might this strained spiritual contrast teach us?

First, there is the majesty of God who covenants with Abram to "give you this land to possess" (Gen. 15:7 RSV). In return, he asks that Abram "walk before me, and be blameless" (Gen. 17:1 RSV). The stubborn children of Israel do not follow, even as the Lord renews his promise: "I am the Lord, I have called you in righteousness" (Isa. 42:6 RSV). How on earth does a majestic God bring a disobedient, pride-filled humanity to himself?

In unfathomable humility God, through Christ, steps into our lives, pays the price of our disobedience, and literally loves us to himself. Christ's humility starts with the incarnation and extends to the cross: "And being found in human form he humbled himself and became obedient unto death, even death on a cross" (Phil. 2:8 rsv). Humility is the remedy because pride is the sickness.

As Augustine wrote, "The one who had such enormous power was hungry, was thirsty . . . was arrested, beaten, crucified and killed. That's the way; proceed along humility, in order to come to eternity. Christ is the home country we are going to; Christ as man is the way we are going by."

Our response to Jesus' humility can only be to come before him in life's most humble posture . . . on our knees, declaring to the world that our risen Lord is a loving, humble God who loves us.

Lord, we come this day acknowledging our pride and your humility, our disobedience and your love. Break us, Lord. Teach us today to be suffering servants, so we may follow your footsteps to our way home.

Atul Tandon is an entrepreneur and author who has worked in consumer banking e-commerce, humanitarian relief, and development in diverse organizations including Citibank, World Vision, and United Way Worldwide. He leads the Tandon Institute, a global social and nonprofit sector accelerator.

First Friday of Lent

BILL LEMKE

❈

GENESIS 22:1–15 • MATTHEW 14:22–32

After these things God tested Abraham. He said to him, "Abraham!"
And he said, "Here I am." He said, "Take your son, your only son
Isaac, whom you love, and go to the land of Moriah, and offer him
there as a burnt offering on one of the mountains that I shall show
you." So Abraham rose early in the morning, saddled his donkey, and
took two of his young men with him, and his son Isaac; he cut the
wood for the burnt offering, and set out and went to the place in the
distance that God had shown him. . . . So Abraham called that place
"The LORD will provide"; as it is said to this day, "On the mount of
the LORD it shall be provided."
Genesis 22:1–3, 14

The Shadow of Death

October 19, 2005: I flew back early from the East Coast because
Brian called me and said that he had cancer. Brian passed away
Thanksgiving Day, November 24, 2005. My only son, seventeen
years old.

My first thoughts were: *How do you love a God who doesn't*
stop the disease and your son dies? God said, "Ask and it shall be
given." He heals people, right? Many people asked, and I begged,
yet Brian died.

I resonate with the Abraham and Isaac story, and I smiled
inside when it was given to me for this meditation. Sitting next
to my son's hospital bed, I cried out to God and said, "Here I am.

I surrender to your will and surrender to whatever happens to Brian." Humility started to take root and grow in me.

God gave his Son as a sacrifice for us because he loves us more than we can imagine. Jesus begged God in the garden to do it some other way, just as I begged God at the hospital. God is not the author of all things but he is the master of all things. In all things in this world, he comes alongside us and says, "I understand." He still does. *Jehovah Jireh*. Whatever way the world has invaded our lives, God says, "I am near; you are not alone." Easter was an event that I believed in, now Easter is the focal, the reality point of my faith.

Lord my God, help us to seek you first and to draw comfort from your peace and from those you put in our lives. Help us rest in you, knowing in our hearts our loved ones are fully in your care. May we humble ourselves and say, "Here I am," then wait and trust in your name Jehovah Jireh—the Provider, Healer, Sustainer, and Companion through this life and into the next. Amen.

Bill Lemke is a man seeking God. He is also the cofounder and executive director of NW Furniture Bank in Tacoma, Washington. His passions include mountaineering, skiing, boating, and spending time with close friends.

First Saturday of Lent

PAULINE FONG

1 KINGS 17:1–10 • MATTHEW 6:9–13

Now Elijah, who was from Tishbe in Gilead, told King Ahab, "As surely as the LORD, the God of Israel, lives—the God I serve—there will be no dew or rain during the next few years until I give the word!" Then the LORD said to Elijah, "Go to the east and hide by Kerith Brook, near where it enters the Jordan River. Drink from the brook and eat what the ravens bring you, for I have commanded them to bring you food." So Elijah did as the LORD told him and camped beside Kerith Brook, east of the Jordan. The ravens brought him bread and meat each morning and evening, and he drank from the brook. But after a while the brook dried up, for there was no rainfall anywhere in the land. Then the LORD said to Elijah, "Go and live in the village of Zarephath, near the city of Sidon. I have instructed a widow there to feed you." So he went to Zarephath. As he arrived at the gates of the village, he saw a widow gathering sticks, and he asked her, "Would you please bring me a little water in a cup?" As she was going to get it, he called to her, "Bring me a bite of bread, too."

1 Kings 17:1–11 (NLT)

A Little Cup of Water

Do you remember what it felt like when you faced and overcame a formidable obstacle in your life? That must have been what Elijah felt as well.

We are first introduced to Elijah as he confronts King Ahab and pronounces God's judgment against the idolatry of Ahab and the kingdom of Israel.

Elijah was God's prophet, and in his confrontation of Ahab, accomplished a significant feat. It ought to have called for celebration. Instead, God sends Elijah to hide in the country, a desolate place, and to become completely dependent and understand God alone is the provider. Then Elijah must depend on the hospitality of a widow, the most humble person in that ancient world economy.

Many of us, if we were in Elijah's place, would be tempted to be angry and complain to God about being sent to a desolate place, or grumble about being dependent on sources not of our choosing. Others of us might be tempted to wonder if God cares, or if he is there at all. And yet, instead of grumbling or complaining, or wondering, Elijah simply did "as the LORD told him" (1 Kings 17:5 NLT).

Humility is not thinking low or bad of ourselves. It is seeing ourselves as God sees us.

In what circumstances do we find ourselves? Are we grumbling or complaining or wondering? Or are we leaning in to listen to God, trusting and deferring to God—even when what we hear may not be what we prefer, even when where we are sent may not be where we desire? Are we humbly doing as the Lord tells us?

We like to think we are in control of life. The reality is, we are fragile and dependent beings. There is freedom in honestly embracing that. Perhaps, as God calls us to be dependent in all circumstances, he calls us to know, in a more real way, who we are. As those who desire to serve him in a deeper way, we are being called to understand who he is, as the living, present, and dependable God.

Gracious God who knows our every need, may
we learn to trust you for our every need and
to know you are our constant companion
and guide in every part of our lives.

Pauline Fong was born and raised in Taipei and immigrated to the United States with her family as a teenager. Pauline graduated from University of California Berkeley with a degree in English literature and a degree from Fuller Seminary in theology. Pauline has worked with InterVarsity Christian Fellowship for twenty-three years, and is the newest member of the M. J. Murdock Charitable Trust team.

The Journey

The path of life takes many turns
to many places, full of grace and
some with Truth.

Each path brings choices to become yourself
and see more clearly.
Distractions litter the path, often appearing
as friends or companions for a journey.
Yet some are designed for ditches or hint
of amusing places to wander off the way.
Still others come to offer words about the path,
born of sorrow, hope, or wizened tears.
They join along, sometimes in person,
some with only journey's hope in common.

The journey calls in whispers too compelling
to ignore, with invitation to hit your stride,
to fill your heart, to fill your lungs for joy's
great cry.
But noise is noise and deafening to whispers and
a focus that would distract from current moment's whim.

Where is the place that joy takes root and
bears its fruit of peace and opens space for
what you are made to do and be?

In part it is found in Galilee where invitations
come at unexpected moments and places.
"Step out, and follow me
you who would dare to journey."

Or as morning dawns and new day breaks the dream,
when new day's hope and promise
invites that move away from comfort.
How strange that the risk to rest
is far greater than that to rise?

The journey is not for timid, tepid souls,
or faint of heart.

It's not for those who seek to settle in safe, secure surroundings or
to hear no discordant notes or,
manage their world in care-filled ways.

Choose journey's paths and partners with greatest care,
and confess in truth you're unprepared, but willing.
This, first steps, clear eyes, and hearts full, focused, and resolute
will guide the way to worlds not yet created and loves beyond
the wildest hope.

Second Week of Lent

Week of Lent

JESUS WALKS

Jesus and His Disciples in the Kidron Valley
by Balage Balogh

Balage Balogh was born in Budapest, Hungary, receiving his education and training in classical art at the Institute of Fine Arts and at the Academy of Fine Arts in Budapest. During the 1990s he began to work with archaeologists and scholars and art historians of the biblical period, Old and New Testaments, so that he might paint scenes from the Bible that were as consistent as possible with the most exacting scholarly understanding of the biblical world, and down to every detail. For this reason, his paintings, or illustrations really, are particularly valued for use in universities, in scholarly journals, in books, and in biblical presentations. To date, his website (www.archaeologyillustrated .com) contains 220 illustrations.

To notice: (1) Recall John 10:4—"When he has driven out all his own, *he walks ahead of them*, and the sheep follow him, because they recognize his voice" (NABRE, emphasis added). Very often in our lives we do not *see* Jesus, but we can learn to *hear* his voice in the Scriptures, in the words or actions of others, or in the writings of the profound Christian tradition. (2) Mark 10:32 reads: "They were on the way, going up to Jerusalem, *and Jesus went ahead of them.* They were amazed, and those who followed were afraid" (NABRE, emphasis added). The artist based his painting on this text. Notice how human it is that his followers—both men and women—hide in different ways their fear (their faces reveal little). Why? Who taught us to do this? (3) Even when one is afraid it is always a good spiritual instinct *to keep walking forward*, staying close with Christ whose mastery is knowing the Way.

© *Balage Balogh, Art Resource, NY*

Second Sunday of Lent

JOHN FRANKLIN

❖

JOB 42:1–6 • LUKE 8:43–48

"My ears had heard of you, but now my eyes have seen you."
Job 42:5 (NIV)

Are You Going to Believe the Author of Your Story?

I have a close friend who has struggled with a chemically imbalanced depression most of his adult life. Every time he tried to wean himself off of his medication in an effort to live a prescription-free life, his depression all too predictably overwhelmed him. During a particularly dark tailspin when he was lamenting his life and questioning why a loving God would allow him to live in such misery, his wife compassionately wrapped her arms around him and whispered into his ear, "Are you going to believe the God of your story?"

Are you going to believe the God of your story? Profoundly, these are the words that have grounded my friend through a life that has been full of "Why God?" questions. He has learned the futility of questioning and the wisdom of simple trust.

This is likewise the lesson of Job. Early on, when Job's life began to fall apart, he had every reason to ask "Why God?" His wealth in ruins, his ten children tragically killed, and his entire body wracked with boils until his sores were infected with worms and his eyes were swollen shut, Job's simple trust was nothing short of amazing. While his closest friends offered their unhelpful counsel regarding *why* Job was suffering (namely, *you suffer because you have sinned*), his wife understandably lamented, "Are you still maintaining your integrity? Curse God and die!" (Job 2:9 NIV). No doubt, it is tempting to be done with God, especially when he is so silent in the midst of our suffering. Job's reply was instructive and revealed the well of his deep trust, "Shall we accept good from God, and not trouble?" (Job 2:10 NIV).

Job believed the God of his story. His friends were transactional—they tried to fix Job's story. Job's posture was transformational—he wanted God more than anything. "Oh, for the days when I was in my prime, when God's intimate friendship blessed my house" (Job 29:4 NIV).

It is understandable that as Job's suffering continued with no relief in sight, he finally wore down and slipped into a several-month stretch demanding to understand why. "Why do you hide your face and consider me your enemy?" (Job 13:24 NIV). God responded by turning the tables on Job and presenting no less than seventy questions right back at him. "Where were you when I laid the earth's foundation?" (Job 38:4 NIV) "Can you bring forth the constellations in their seasons?" (Job 38:32 NIV). "Do you know the laws of the heavens?" (Job 38:33 NIV). Job's lesson: it's never wrong to be angry with God and express our frustration; but, who are we to criticize God's plans or tell God what he should do? Job was reminded: stop trying to figure out *why* and simply believe the Author of your story.

For a brief period Job had fallen into his friends' transactional approach to God. But in the end, Job was brought back to a transformational posture, culminating with him realizing, "My ears had heard of you, but now my eyes have seen you" (Job 42:5 NIV).

Or as one theologian translates the passage, "By hearsay my ears have heard of you, but now my eyes have seen you."

To be sure, until we enter into deep suffering, it is possible to live on the secondhand hearsay of God. We are comforted by stories of how he has met others in their darkest days. But when the bottom falls out in our own story, mere hearsay no longer meets the need. Our soul cries out to know nothing less than his very presence. Suffering draws us into a whole new depth of knowing him. It explains why the apostle Paul would write from his prison cell in Philippi the virtue of not only knowing Christ in the power of his resurrection, but likewise in "the fellowship of his sufferings, being made conformable unto his death;" (Phil. 3:10 kjv).

Considering Job's lesson, I must reflect and ask myself, *How much do I really know God versus living by mere hearsay?* And what is my posture in suffering? Does my lament drive me to demand to know *why* or does it draw me into a deeper belief in the God of my story?

Are you going to believe the Author of your story?

Jesus, as we walk with you and look in to your face, we realize we see the face of God. Help us to trust you with our story and our lives.

John Franklin and his wife, Staci, live in Beaverton, Oregon. They have three sons and three awesome daughters-in-law. John is a program director of the M. J. Murdock Charitable Trust.

Second Monday of Lent

KATE HARRIS

❧

MATTHEW 1:1–17 • COLOSSIANS 1:15–20

He is the image of the invisible God, the firstborn of all creation; for in him all things in heaven and on earth were created, things visible and invisible, whether thrones or dominions or rulers or powers—all things have been created through him and for him. He himself is before all things, and in him all things hold together. He is the head of the body, the church; he is the beginning, the firstborn from the dead, so that he might come to have first place in everything. For in him all the fullness of God was pleased to dwell, and through him God was pleased to reconcile to himself all things, whether on earth or in heaven, by making peace through the blood of his cross.
Colossians 1:15–20

Limitations and Possibilities

A lawyer friend of mine once told me that early in his clerkship he left the remains of his lunch on a court cafeteria table in a rush to get to his next meeting. In his haste he left a folder behind. When he returned to retrieve it, he found his boss, a justice on the U.S. Supreme Court, clearing the table and wiping it down for an elderly tourist to sit.

In its own way, this journey in the days of Lent invites the same kind of reflection this moment offered my friend. It invites us to consider ourselves honestly in light of the goodness of someone far more powerful than we are. Through our practices of prayer, reflection, and personal discipline, God invites us to contend with our own limitations with the welcome assurance that he is before all things and holding them all together.

And yet, despite his place as Lord, Christ demonstrates the power in kindness. He didn't have to dwell with man, or reconcile all things, or bring peace by death. It wasn't expected. But he chose to do it.

My friend recalls being forever changed by this lunch table episode. He has since dedicated years to knowing and serving this same Supreme Court justice. In their way, Lent and Easter invite the same transformational perspective for us. As Brother Lawrence writes, "We should feed and nourish our souls with high notions of God, which would yield us great joy in being devoted to him."

Father, Son, and Holy Spirit, thank you for showing your power in love and guide me in how to do the same with the particular influence and resources you have entrusted to me this day. Grant that I would grow daily in my love for you and in my love for others. Grant me, by your power, the same pleasure you take in reconciling and making peace with those around me. Amen.

Kate Harris is a writer and consultant in Washington, DC. She is wife to a good man and mother to their four young children.

Second Tuesday of Lent

CHUCK SCHLIMPERT

*In the beginning was the Word, and the Word was with God, and
the Word was God. He was in the beginning with God.
All things were made through Him, and without Him
nothing was made that was made. In Him was life, and the life
was the light of men. And the light shines in the darkness, and the
darkness did not comprehend it. . . . And the Word became flesh and
dwelt among us, and we beheld His glory, the glory as of the only
begotten of the Father, full of grace and truth.*
John 1:1–5, 14 (NKJV)

A Corporate Communion

I love Starbucks. Hard to believe it hasn't been around forever.
It arrived in 1971, seeking to be "a third space," a place where
community, friendship, and reflection could take place in addition to great coffee.

Interestingly, there is a group that has sought to be a place for
community, friendship, and connection for more than two thousand years. It's called the church—the people of God gathered.
In addition to some pretty good coffee, the church around the
world has sought to serve, remind, and reflect the reality that
God desires to be present in your world and mine.

God's Word, especially his Word for this day, however, is encouraging, uplifting, and eternal. His love for us has not changed. We simply have a new set of circumstances in which to experience and share God's love. As people continue to yearn for community, we have ample opportunity to demonstrate God's glory and his love for us. When we look into the eyes of the ones we love, when a child we have helped feed or learn to read holds our hand, then together we behold his glory! And we have the opportunity to share our faith in community as well. The Word still seeks to become flesh each and every day, through you and me. Let it be so.

Gracious and loving God, I thank you for the love you have shown and the blessing it is to be part of your family. I pray you would bless all that I do and say this day so I may bring glory to your name and bring hope to those don't yet know your love. In the name of Jesus, amen.

Charles Schlimpert serves as president of Concordia University in Portland, Oregon. Now in his thirty-third year as president, he is the longest tenured college or university president in the Pacific Northwest.

Second Wednesday of Lent

DOUG NUENKE

✳

LUKE 1:39–56 • MATTHEW 4:1–17

"His mercy extends to those who fear him,
from generation to generation.
He has performed mighty deeds with his arm;
he has scattered those who are proud in their inmost thoughts.
He has brought down rulers from their thrones
but has lifted up the humble."
Luke 1:50–52 (NIV)

Then Jesus was led by the Spirit into the wilderness to be tempted by
the devil. After fasting forty days and forty nights, he was hungry.
Matthew 4:1–2 (NIV)

The Power of Submission

We live in a world that often cheers pride and independence. God's kingdom purposes head a different direction.

These days of Lent help us reflect on the "God came to earth" story, the values that form the foundation for our lives, and his desire to live through us.

Our reading today from Luke 1 includes words from Mary, the mother of Jesus. This unsuspecting but trustworthy teenager speaks of a primary attribute of God's kingdom: humility. What a counter-cultural value for power brokers and those of us who like to control things, then or now. We even see it in the womb God chose to cradle the soon-to-be Savior of the world—a poor, unwed teen. Humility embodied!

In the passage from Matthew, we see the words, "Jesus was led." The Son of God spent his time on earth being led from place to place, seeking and submitting himself to do the will of God, being led by the Holy Spirit. He was sent to earth by the authority of his Father. His parents had to *flee* to Egypt under threat of death. He experienced betrayal, being *led* to a cross to die. In Matthew 4, Jesus is *led by God's Spirit* to forty days of hunger and temptation.

In each case, Jesus humbly submitted to his Father's desires. His life displayed humility—a kind of openness and purposefulness that affected all he did. It also modeled an acceptance of God's plans, even when it caused pain, and eventually took his life. And he did it with one end in mind—for our sakes.

Can we learn and follow in this same humble way, as followers of Jesus and for the sake of those yet to know him? What might that look like for us this day? What might this look like during this time in which we live?

Lord Jesus, as we reflect on your life, and your willingness to be led by your Father and his plans, help us to have the same spirit of submission. We like control and we prefer to be in charge. We open our hands, loosen our grip, and say "yes" to your ways. Show us where we are holding too tightly to our wants and desires and where we need to let go, so we can serve others and love you more fully.

Doug Nuenke serves as the U.S. president of The Navigators®, a ministry that helps people be disciples of Jesus in every walk of life. He loves interacting with friends and family about the life and ways of Jesus.

Second Thursday of Lent

MATT MIKALATOS

❦

LUKE 2: 1–21 • MATTHEW 5:1–11

But Mary treasured all these words and pondered them in her heart.
Luke 2:19

Power in Every Word

When Mary heard the shepherds' story of celestial annunciation, she gathered those words like unruly children and brought them to order. She collected them like beautiful stones from a riverbed, and lined them up, still damp from the river, and watched as the sun baked them dry. Every word, every whisper of communication from God, was something to be cherished, hidden away, treasured, remembered. Especially because these words were about her beloved Jesus.

Words make the world. God spoke light into being, and also land and animals and plants, the stars, the sun, the moon. All through his words. Words have power to enlighten, to empower, to create, and to destroy. They should be treated with respect, used with care.

Mary gathered words like stones, turning them over and over in her mind until the rough edges fell away, until they became smooth and polished and permanent. All so she could know, so she could remember each promise, every description of Jesus, the Savior of the world, God himself, her beloved, dear child.

Christ himself is the first Word, the one who was in the beginning and who is with God and also is God. He is the living Word. And he became the Word made flesh. He is the Word who exists, present in the beginning, spoken beyond the end. He is God putting on human flesh. God made understandable. God with us.

Like Mary, let us gather this Word into our hearts. Let us treasure him and ponder him. Let us remember him and honor him, and be amazed.

> *Living Word of God, speak to us. Remain in our hearts and bring to mind all the things you have promised, all the hoped-for futures, all the divine communications you have blessed us with over the years. Let us be filled up with you, and may our own words come from the overflow of your presence in our hearts.*

Matt Mikalatos is the author of several books, the most recent of which is *Sky Lantern*. He and his wife, Krista, serve with Cru in Portland, Oregon.

Second Friday of Lent

TOM BEAUMONT

❊

ISAIAH 42:1–4 • MATTHEW 16:5–28

"Here is my servant, whom I uphold, my chosen one
in whom I delight; I will put my Spirit on him,
and he will bring justice to the nations."
Isaiah 42:1 (NIV)

"For the Son of Man is going to come in his Father's glory
with his angels, and then he will reward each person
according to what they have done."
Matthew 16:27 (NIV)

Let Justice Roll Down

Where are you, justice? I'm not seeing much evidence of you these days. I'm not asking for much, maybe just a glimpse of what is "right" or "fair" once in a while. I've got to admit, your absence is turning me into a pessimist—a "glass half empty" kind of person—and I don't like it. All I am seeing is that God is being ignored, truth is being redefined or twisted, and demonstrations of your presence seem to be few and far between in the places I live.

The prophet Isaiah announced that when the chosen Messiah comes, "he will bring justice to the nations" (Isa. 42:1 NIV). Launched from the very faithfulness of God you were to be on your way to do what justice does, to bring hope and a measure of righteous order to our world. But instead the Christ was met by a Law that was perverted and religious elitists who took matters of moral conduct into their own misguided hands.

Yet, it was that same Christ who made it clear that a time is indeed coming when he will return in the glory of his Father and will "reward each person according to what they have done" (Matt. 16:27 NIV). Maybe, then, you (justice) are more about introspection than retribution. Perhaps you are best served in our hearts, and our search for you best done inwardly than outwardly. I suspect it is there I will find you. Maybe what I need to do is take responsibility for my life, my community, my work, and my friends. Maybe justice, like love and hope, begins with me.

Dear Father, there is a time coming when you will right all wrongs and your justice will prevail, and for that we must patiently wait. But in our waiting may our eyes turn first to ourselves to look at our own hearts. May our motives and intentions be revealed, and may we become the person you created each of us to be, living in the world as you would have us. May our deeds be aligned to your purposes. Thy will be done on earth as it is in heaven. Grant us your grace until that day. Amen.

Tom Beaumont is the executive director of The Firs, a camp and retreat center in Bellingham, Washington, where he has served for thirty-one years. He and his wife, Mary, have been married for almost thirty-seven years, and they have three grown children.

Second Saturday of Lent

RON FRANK

❁

LUKE 23:26–49 • PSALM 33:20–22

"Father, forgive them, for they don't know what they are doing."
"I assure you, today you will be with me in paradise."
"Father, I entrust my spirit into your hands!"
Luke 23:34, 43, 46 (NLT)

The Cost of Forgiveness

In the midst of experiencing the most brutal form of execution ever devised by man, Jesus' final words as recorded in Luke tell us much about what—or, more importantly, *whom*—he was thinking during those hours of pain, separation, and, ultimately, physical death. I believe he was thinking about us—you and me—for in these three short phrases lie the heart of the gospel.

First, in asking his Father to forgive them (Roman soldiers, Jewish leaders, politicians) for putting him to death, Jesus points to our own need for forgiveness too. We share the responsibility for his death, and desperately need a Savior to redeem us from our sin. Jesus willingly gave up his life so that we can have life, now and for eternity. Forgiveness through faith in Jesus' finished work on the cross—the heart of the gospel shared with words and blood for you and me. *Forgiveness.*

Second, Jesus' response to a dying criminal's request to be remembered in his kingdom clearly demonstrates that our deeds can't save us. For Jesus' reply, "you will be with me in paradise" (Luke 23:43 NLT), indicates that salvation is by faith alone in Christ alone (and that it's never too late!). *Faith.*

Finally, as the curtain that closed off the Holy of Holies was torn from top to bottom; and as Jesus, in ultimate control, entrusts his spirit to the Father, he loudly proclaims that his work is finished. The barrier between God and man is split, making it possible for each of us to connect with God directly—and only—through our Savior, Jesus. *Finished.*

> *Father, thanks for giving us a glimpse of Jesus'*
> *mind and heart as he experienced a most painful*
> *death—that he thought about our need for*
> *forgiveness; that salvation is by faith alone and*
> *not something we can earn; that his finished work*
> *gives us direct access to you. What a Savior! Amen.*

Ron Frank serves as the Pacific Northwest region vice president of field ministry for the Fellowship of Christian Athletes. He's been married to his best friend, Val, for thirty-three years, and they have three grown children.

Third
Week of Lent

REPENTANCE

Saint John the Baptist
by Domenikos Theotokopoulos or "El Greco" (1541–1614)

El Greco was born in one of the cradles of Western civilization, the Island of Crete, but was to become one of the foremost painters of Spain. He moved to Venice in his early twenties to study under Titian; then to Rome, to work amidst the community of the best painters there; and finally moved permanently to Toledo, Spain, in his thirty-fifth year (1576). Through his technique of elongating human figures, his use of brilliant cold light, and his preference for deep brown and olive coloring, he developed a singular capacity to "enhance the expressive intensity and supernatural character of the scenes."[4]

To notice: (1) John grows thinner and thinner. Why? Because at John 3:30: "That is why my happiness is now complete. He must grow greater and greater and I less and less" (PHILLIPS). (2) Though John is so physically thin—and the elongation of the figure makes this more apparent—his muscles are toned and strongly defined. He is simultaneously an image of striking weakness and formidable strength, an image of meekness and fierceness. (3) Toward whom is the Baptist looking, and with such a compassionate and vulnerable face? He is looking away from both the Lamb-Christ and the cross against which he appears to lean.

Album/Art Resource, NY

Third Sunday of Lent

RICK GANZ

✤

MARK 1:4–8

*John [the] Baptist appeared in the desert proclaiming a baptism of
repentance for the forgiveness of sins. People of the whole Judean
countryside and all the inhabitants of Jerusalem were going out to
him and were being baptized by him in the Jordan River
as they acknowledged their sins.*
Mark 1:4 (NABRE)

A Worthy Repentance

The Gospel of Mark opens with the arrival into the wilderness
of the last prophet of the Old Testament. John is the image *par
excellence* for our third week of Lent, because the repentance he
announced actually did open a way for the coming of the Lord.

The Baptist knew how to open in people a way for Christ to
enter through the skillful manner in which he simultaneously
invited and demanded repentance for the forgiveness of sins.
Many today do not know how to do this, whose manner of
proclaiming repentance actually occludes the way of Christ in
the souls of people, turning them in on themselves (*incurvatus in
se*)[5] in the same way that sin does. Often the call to repentance
is done in such a way that it traps people in their sin rather than
opening a way for them to permanently let go of their sin.

We have been taught that repentance is *necessary*. Perhaps that
is not all? Something else is necessary, such that, having that,

true repentance becomes *inevitable*. "What do you want me to do for you?" He said, "Lord, let me see again" (Mark 10:51 NABRE).

Think of that lovely line from A. W. Tozer: "Man is bored, because he is too *big* to be happy with that which sin is giving him."[6] Tozer understood that true repentance assumes a prior experience of how big we have been created by God to be—"Yet you have made them a little lower than God, and crowned them with glory and honor" (Heb. 2:7 NABRE). If that *largeness* of created gift is shown us, effectively evoked in us, by those calling us to repentance, then the *smallness* of our choices reveal themselves for what they are—as our *sins* against the gift. At least in that moment of being awakened to the truth of the gift, repentance is inevitable. It is what we *want* more than anything else.

I recall here a conviction articulated, and often repeated, by that remarkable Oregon athlete, a runner, Steve Prefontaine (1951–1975): "To give anything less than your best is to sacrifice the gift."

John the Baptist must have been able to preach repentance in God's way—the huge crowds who came out to hear him and to be baptized by him (including Jesus) prove it. Each person experienced anew his or her inalienable dignity as a child of God. John was able to paint in their imaginations a compelling image of a people made in the very image and likeness of God—them!—such that each one knew how *small* he or she had been living out his or her life. And they, having experienced John himself, that fierce and completely credible man, whose single-hearted love for God was so palpably evident, they found their repentance becoming inevitable. And so to him standing in the river they came; thousands came. The Baptist knew how to open a way in people for "the dear Christ [to enter] in."[7]

What is *necessary* for true repentance is for us to have a fresh, and ever-renewed, experience of the extraordinary gift God created us to be for each other and for the whole created world. Without this experience evoked in us by the profound people among us, but most especially by Jesus—the way the Father loved and awakened his beloved Son!—then all *necessary* repentance becomes for people a dreary exercise in self-reproach and self-absorption. Such a congregation of haunted people is pleasing only to the people who have no need of repentance, but not to God.

> *Dear Father, awaken us as you did the Baptist, who was sent, in the fullness of time, to awaken us to our forgotten dignity as your own children, into whom you have poured some of creation's most profound gifts. Make our repentance inevitable.*

Rick Ganz is a member of the Society of Jesus, the Jesuits, and is the head of the Faber Institute.

Third Monday of Lent

JESS BIELMAN

❀

PSALM 25 • MARK 2:1–5

Make me to know your ways, O LORD; teach me your paths. Lead me in your truth, and teach me, for you are the God of my salvation; for you I wait all day long. Be mindful of your mercy, O LORD, and of your steadfast love, for they have been from of old. Do not remember the sins of my youth or my transgressions; according to your steadfast love remember me, for your goodness' sake, O LORD!
Psalm 25:4–7

Free From "Do-Goodism"

I have spent most of my Christian life thinking of repentance only in terms of the turning away of personal sins. Through recent events in our nation and the world I have been challenged to think of sin in a personal way as well as in systemic, societal, and within our cultural times.

If sin can be understood as a wider concept, then repentance could be as well. The implication is that maybe repentance is less a one-time turning away from bad behavior and more a lifestyle headed in the opposite ways of the sins of our times. Materialism, racism, busyness, or self-importance are soul-damaging characteristics that often infect every culture. We ought to recognize and seek to live with an intentional resistance. Repentance becomes a daily act of leaning on God for new life in the midst of a corruption of the spirit that often comes in ways we do not even realize at first.

In Psalm 25:4 the psalmist pleads, "Make me to know your ways, O LORD; teach me your path." By verse 18 he begs, "forgive all my sins." This is the path of Lent. Often our need for guidance is a trail that leads to a deeper understanding of our sin. Between these phrases is a radical life reorientation away from fear and loneliness toward virtues of humility and trust.

What if we focused less on what we were turning from and more toward the prophetic virtues of God's kingdom we were turning toward?

*Lord, help us flee from the way the world
seeks to shape and mold us. Teach us your
ways, and take away these distractions that
so easily entangle us. Lead us more fully
into your grace, goodness, and freedom.*

Jess Bielman teaches and directs Christian Ministries at Warner Pacific College. He is an ordained minister in the Church of God (Anderson, Indiana), copastor of a house church in Southeast Portland, husband, and the proud father of two little girls.

Third Tuesday of Lent

GREG JOHNSON

❈

PSALM 41 • LUKE 18:35–43

Happy are those who consider the poor;
the LORD delivers them in the day of trouble.
Psalm 41:1

A Severe Mercy

As I reflect on the similarities of David in Psalm 41 and the blind beggar found in Luke 18:35–43, I recognize our ever-present need for mercy.

Adversity comes in many forms, yet our hope in Christ sustains us. David's cry for mercy and repentance has its source in his despair, illness, and broken relationships, including his rejection of his best friend. The blind beggar's cry came from his deep desire to have his sight restored. However, most importantly, Christ himself gave us an incredible example and connection with mercy through his life. His passion and death gave us an example of what it means to cry out faithfully, trusting the mercy of his Father for his Son.

A cry for mercy typically comes with a heart of surrender. I have experienced a strong sense of God's mercy in the high country when I observed there the rawness of life, the constant fight for survival and control, and this collision between dependency and trust in God and on others. My need for mercy also comes within my own family, where chronic health issues have given me a better appreciation of what it feels like to be powerless (like David).

I am often reminded as I serve in leadership roles, that mercy is about losing my tight-fisted grip so Christ can take my hand. With that, the less control I feel I have, the more dependent on Christ I become. So whether a king, a beggar, or somewhere in between, we are never too important or lowly to cry out for mercy, to repent, and to seek restoration from our King, Lord, and Savior. Reflect and receive God's mercies for you in this day!

God of mercy, I repent of my attempt to rely on my own strength, knowledge, and capacities to control, knowing too little of your sufficient grace and mercy. Please God, breathe life into me that I may also extend grace and mercy to others. Amen.

Greg Johnson is the director of Stonewater Ranch (a branch of Youth Dynamics) in Leavenworth, Washington, where he lives with his wife, Ursula, and three of their four children.

Third Wednesday of Lent

KIMMY STOKESBARY

❊

ISAIAH 43 • JOHN 8:1–11

Do not fear, for I have redeemed you; I have called you by name,
you are mine. . . . For I am the LORD your God,
the Holy One of Israel, your Savior.
Isaiah 43:1b–3a

You Are Precious
in My Sight

Adam and Eve disobeyed God and ate from the tree in the middle of the garden. And then, having eaten, Adam and Eve realized that they were naked and hid from God.

From then on, because of sin, humanity could not experience the intimate relationship with God that Adam and Eve had first experienced in the garden. But God longs for relationship, and so God chooses Israel to be God's people.

But they, too, fail. They sin and rebel. And they go astray.

So God sends the Babylonians to overthrow Israel and carry the people into exile.

Rejected.

Despised.

But in Isaiah 43:4 God speaks a different message to them, "[Y]ou are precious in my sight, and honored, and I love you."

"I, I am He who blots out your transgression for my own sake, and I will not remember your sins" (v. 25).

This is an astonishing message. They are not rejected and despised, but loved, cherished, and even forgiven by the very God who created them.

And there's more, even in Babylon when they feel the furthest from God, God is still with them.

And so the good news is that no matter our past, no matter where we've been or where we find ourselves, God continues to call us back to relationship.

Over and over in the Bible this story is told. What incredible news! How could we forget?

In this Lenten season, may we repent and return to God. And so receive our identity, not as those who are rejected and despised, but as those who are loved and cherished by God.

*God, so often we see ourselves only as sinners—
broken, rejected, and even despised. And yet you
call us your beloved. You regularly, faithfully,
creatively, and powerfully remind us over and
over—we are loved! May we hear and believe
the identity you give us and may we turn back
to you this day and every day to come. Amen.*

Kimmy Stokesbary is a former intern at Camp Lutherhaven in the M. J. Murdock Charitable Trust Vision and Call program, a graduate of Princeton Theological Seminary, and currently an associate pastor at the Clairmont Presbyterian Church in Atlanta, Georgia.

Third Thursday of Lent

AMY MUIA

DEUTERONOMY 8:2–10 • MATTHEW 11:25–30

*At that time Jesus said, "I thank you, Father, Lord of heaven and
earth, because you have hidden these things from the wise
and the intelligent and have revealed them to infants;
yes, Father, for such was your gracious will. All things have been
handed over to me by my Father; and no one knows the Son
except the Father, and no one knows the Father except
the Son and anyone to whom the Son chooses to reveal him.
Come to me, all you that are weary and are carrying heavy burdens,
and I will give you rest. Take my yoke upon you, and learn from
me; for I am gentle and humble in heart, and you will find rest
for your souls. For my yoke is easy, and my burden is light."*
Matthew 11:25–30

Maintaining the Low

In our weekly Bible studies at the Skagit County Jail, we often
sing a song inspired by 1 Corinthians 1 and Matthew 11 with the
inmates:

You choose what is low and despised
to reveal your ways to the wise
You choose the weak
to bring low the kingdoms and the powers
for this was your good pleasure.

The inmates and addicts we work with take great comfort in Jesus' words, echoed by Paul in 1 Corinthians 1:26–30:

> Consider your own call, brothers and sisters: not many of you were wise by human standards, not many were powerful, not many were of noble birth. But God chose what is foolish in the world to shame the wise; God chose what is weak in the world to shame the strong; God chose what is low and despised in the world, things that are not, to reduce to nothing things that are, so that no one might boast in the presence of God. He is the source of your life in Christ Jesus, who became for us wisdom from God . . .

What a great comfort! We qualify. We hear the call of God to renounce our self-important ways, our human wisdom. We repent, and thus become like children—in fact, like infants. The only thing an infant can do is cry out; she is completely at the mercy of her caregiver. And the Divine Caregiver is gentle and humble in heart. We rest. We take on the yoke of utter dependence and waiting, and we see the face of God.

As much as we like to consider ourselves powerful, in control, or masters of our world, we are not. We enter the world as powerless, dependent babies. And most of us will leave the world as powerless, dependent older people. In between, we do well to learn the reality of depending on Christ.

Father, we thank you that in the place of dependence, you reveal yourself to us. Wash us clean of our self-reliance. We choose the light and easy yoke you offer us, and yield up the heavy yokes we have been carrying. Keep us today in your peace, like an infant at rest.

Amy Muia is a minister with the Evangelical Covenant Church; a chaplain in the Skagit County Jail; and the founder and codirector of New Earth Recovery, where she and her husband, Alan, direct homes for men and women in recovery from drug and alcohol addiction.

Third Friday of Lent

PAMELA HAVEY LAU

❧

DEUTERONOMY 9:13–25 • JOHN 4:1–26

"God is spirit, and those who worship him
must worship in spirit and truth."
John 4:24

A Worthy Worship

I often ask myself, *Why can't I live the life I long for—the life of constant communication with God? Why is my heart so dark, so cold? Where's the light of Christ burning bright in me?* Only one thing can help me: I must weep bitterly for my sin, for my turning away from what God shows me and doing what I want. The life I long for, the life of worship in spirit and truth, comes as a gift when I boldly repent with heart-wrenching conviction the sin that is blocking my heart. I must stop complaining and saying, *I will do better next time because God understands.*

I begin by praying to our Lord Jesus, who is alive and interceding for us at this very moment, and confess bad moods, pride, jealousy, envy, unkind judgments, unforgiving thoughts and acts, hatred for my brother or sister, or even myself. Whatever is brought to my mind, I confess, and I hear the gentle, graceful voice of my Savior say, "You are right when you say . . ."

A deeper repentance happens as you and I bow low in his presence, asking for more of his Spirit and more of his truth. The turning point in our lives comes as the Lord reveals to us our self-confidence, self-will, and self-pleasing. Will we give these things up for a closer relationship with the One who seeks to deliver us through his greatness?

Repentance is our pathway to the powerful life we need and want. N. T. Wright observes that when sin is confessed, resurrection power of any kind is not far behind.

Almighty God, you overcame death through Jesus, your Son, and opened a path for me to know you and you to know me forever. I ask that you would give me deep joy this resurrection week as you raise me from the death of sin by your life-giving Spirit. I'm alive because Jesus is alive and reigning with you.

Pamela Havey Lau is the author of *A Friend in Me* and *Soul Strength*. She is also a graduate of Liberty University and Colorado State University, a professor at George Fox University, and a conference speaker. Pamela is married to Brad Lau, and they live near Portland, Oregon, with their three daughters.

Third Saturday of Lent

PAUL YOUNG

❦

2 SAMUEL 22:17–51 • GALATIANS 4:1–7

*And because you are children, God has sent the Spirit of his Son into
our hearts, crying, "Abba! Father!"*
Galatians 4:6

An Inheritance
for the Ages

We have forgotten where and what is our home and identity.
As children we knew, once upon a time, before the wars around
us pressed us into the molds of conformity and the complexity
of adulthood drove for control, and took from us the memory of
what is true, and beautiful, and good, and wondrous.

These passages are about repentance; not re-penancing (paying
a performance price for our inheritance), but the turning and
transformation of the whole person back to the Truth.

When we lost our innocence and became childish adults,
our responses, like David's, became full of narcissistic fury,
projecting on God our gloating sense of personal vindication
and self-righteous joy at the retributive and punitive justice that

seemed to fall upon those we disliked. We forgot that the roads we traveled ourselves were filled with depression and failure.

Childish, we were imprisoned; lost to the truth of our inheritance as children of God and under every law that we imagined would free us, but which only perpetuated the lie that we are slaves.

There is a timing to the activity of God that releases us into our inheritance, the truth of our home and identity. The cosmic timing is the incarnation of Jesus, the Son, in whom we were created and have always had our dwelling and being, but we had forgotten. Then there is personal timing, unique to each when the Father, ignoring our performance, kisses us, dresses us, and restores our memory.

> *Abba, thank you for waiting while I am lost*
> *in a far country. And when I turn toward*
> *you and come running back, and lift up my*
> *face from the shame that covers me, you kiss*
> *me and tell me again the truth of who I am*
> *and to whom I have always belonged.*

Paul Young: son, husband, father, "Gramps," friend, longtime writer but accidental author, Third Culture Kid (MK), stumbler, hugger, grateful, forever found, kind, pure of heart, living inside the grace of one day and in the embrace of relentless affirmation.

Grip of Grace

The journey of life
brings opportunities disguised as
choices and roads full
of bumps and curves and
unexpected places.

Navigation is both art and craft,
best honed
through watchful eye and listening heart
to one who sees the whole terrain

Some paths bring
light and unimagined worlds,
while other ways overpromise and
give way to detours and dead ends.

The grip of grace is there,
constant companion,
patient guide,
offered by one who loves
both journey and pilgrim.

Fourth Week OF Lent

LAMENT

Peter the Apostle
by Anthony van Dyck (1599–1641)

This Flemish painter, draughtsman, and etcher has been judged the equal of that artistic genius Peter Paul Rubens (see Week 7), who was twenty-two years his senior and in whose studio in Antwerp van Dyck studied, and with whom he would be compared as a painter all his life. He began at age ten to study painting at Antwerp's Guild of St. Luke and was judged a "master" by age nineteen. He had a particular gift for painting portraits; "His fame as a portrait painter in the cities of the southern Netherlands, as well as in London, Genoa, Rome, and Palermo, has never been outshone."[8]

To notice: (1) The gesture of Peter's right hand (perhaps the very hand he reached toward Jesus as he began to drown in the sea—"Lord, save me!" (Matt. 14:30 NABRE) suggests that Peter is owning up, Peter who had betrayed his Lord. No longer "Is it I, Lord?" of the Last Supper (see Matthew 26:22); rather, "It *is* I, Lord." (2) When one is feeling intensely one's personal failure, which tears open a space in the soul through which the evil spirit can pour shame, it is almost always the case that he or she lets fall his or her head and face, unable to look up. Peter's profoundly expressive eyes reveal his lament, yet he keeps his head and face up, looking toward God. See Psalm 34:6, "Look to him and be radiant, and your faces may not blush for shame" (NABRE).

HIP/Art Resource, NY

Fourth Sunday of Lent

SHAWNA GORDON AND STEVE MOORE

❖

PSALM 63:1–8 • 1 JOHN 1:8–9

O God, you are my God, I seek you,
my soul thirsts for you;
my flesh faints for you,
as in a dry and weary land where there is no water.
So I have looked upon you in the sanctuary,
beholding your power and glory.
Because your steadfast love is better than life,
my lips will praise you.
So I will bless you as long as I live;
I will lift up my hands and call on your name.
My soul is satisfied as with a rich feast,
and my mouth praises you with joyful lips
when I think of you on my bed,
and meditate on you in the watches of the night;
for you have been my help,
and in the shadow of your wings I sing for joy.
My soul clings to you;
your right hand upholds me.
Psalm 63:1–8

God Wastes No Pain

To take on the posture of lament is not an easy one. At its core, lament is the action to deeply grieve and to feel the heaviness of sorrow. We would be so bold as to say that our culture, both Christian and not, does not embrace grief or loss or pain very well. We like to rush past pain, eager to get back to normal.

In times of loss, for example at a funeral, we are so quick to say, "But they are in a better place now, so rejoice!" While this may be true, we have seen richness in sitting in the grief; in recognizing and naming the pain and the hurt. Jesus modeled this well, as he did not simply rush past pain or sadness, but truly entered into them. He allowed the weight of grief to move him into places of compassion and care. Pain is often the tool God uses to lead us to become the person he created us to be. It can be a path to wholeness.

To lament isn't easy, and it often makes us uncomfortable. It is unnatural, but a true reality of living in a broken world. It is necessary to grieve; to recognize that we cannot do everything on our own and, as silly as it may sound, welcome the care of others. To experience deep sorrow is to trust the God that sees us and holds us; that goes before us and walks beside us. This is the God that stands at the bedside of the lowly, grieving alongside us with a Father's heart.

He will not abandon us. There is nothing we encounter that God will not take and weave into a pattern for our ultimate good.

Jesus, teach us to enter into the uncomfortable spaces that draw us closer to you. Where grief can blind us, show us your grace and love through those you bring around us, acting as your hands and feet. May we lean into your care and comfort. In the places of pain and sorrow, teach us to find rest in the truth that you are with us in the midst of it all.

Shawna Gordon is a graduate of George Fox University (GFU) who now serves as the chaplain for the women's basketball team at GFU. She is also the pastor of Youth and Families at North Valley Friends Church in Newberg, Oregon.

Steve and his wife, Thanne, have four adult children, Madison and Chandi, Maegan and Mollie. Steve works at the M. J. Murdock Charitable Trust.

Fourth Monday of Lent

JEFF GREENMAN

❅

JOB 2:11–13 • 1 CORINTHIANS 13; 8–12

Now when Job's three friends heard of all these troubles that had come upon him, each of them set out from his home—Eliphaz the Temanite, Bildad the Shuhite, and Zophar the Naamathite. They met together to go and console and comfort him. When they saw him from a distance, they did not recognize him, and they raised their voices and wept aloud; they tore their robes and threw dust in the air upon their heads. They sat with him on the ground seven days and seven nights, and no one spoke a word to him, for they saw that his suffering was very great.
Job 2:11–13

What Companion Will You Be?

The story of Job is synonymous with undeserved, mysterious, and profound suffering. He is a prominent, wealthy person who is "blameless" and "upright" (Job 1:1). He is enduring the loss of his animals (a source of wealth), the tragic death of his ten children, as well as a debilitating skin disease. Amidst this great suffering, he does not blame God for his calamities, though he cannot understand.

Three far-flung friends appear in the story. They agree together to comfort Job. The friends collaborate on an intentional, sacrificial mission of spiritual friendship. Their goal is simply to "console and comfort him" (Job 2:11). Entering into his pain and loss, they weep aloud, tear their robes, and cover themselves with dust, a symbolic way of saying, "Job, we are in it with you." They literally come alongside Job, sitting on the ground with him, a place of honesty and humility. "We, too, cannot understand and do not know what to say."

Remarkably, they express their compassion and comfort without saying a single word. Later in Job's story, we find these friends being very talkative, giving questionable and unhelpful advice. But they are at their best when they simply come alongside. Sometimes it is best to say little and just be there.

Sometimes we feel uncomfortable with silence. We feel pressure to say something wise, helpful, or healing. During these days of Lent, we can ask ourselves who would be comforted and encouraged by our mere presence. Has God placed someone in our circle of friends who needs our support and encouragement, perhaps even without saying all the right words?

Lord God, soften our hearts to the pain others around us may have. By your Spirit, make us attentive and compassionate friends, that we might bring comfort, hope, and presence to those in need. We ask this through Jesus Christ, our Lord. Amen.

Jeff Greenman is president and professor of theology and ethics at Regent College, Vancouver, British Columbia, Canada. His research, writing, and teaching have focused on Christian ethics, spiritual formation, leadership development, and theological education.

Fourth Tuesday of Lent

PETE C. MENJARES

❀

PSALM 4:1–8 • LUKE 8:40–48

Answer me when I call, O God of my right!
You gave me room when I was in distress.
Be gracious to me, and hear my prayer.
How long, you people, shall my honor suffer shame?
How long will you love vain words, and seek after lies? Selah
But know that the Lord has set apart the faithful for himself;
the Lord hears when I call to him.
When you are disturbed, do not sin;
ponder it on your beds, and be silent. Selah
Offer right sacrifices,
and put your trust in the LORD.
There are many who say, "O that we might see some good!
Let the light of your face shine on us, O LORD!"
You have put gladness in my heart
more than when their grain and wine abound.
I will both lie down and sleep in peace;
for you alone, O LORD, make me lie down in safety.
Psalm 4

Opening the Depths of Our Soul

Lament, it seems, is a neglected subject in nearly every community. Yet, consistently, lament is honestly present within many people's lives in the Bibles.

The author of the psalm knew the pain of life and of lament that comes with pain:

"Answer me when I call, O God of my right!
You gave me room when I was in distress.
Be gracious to me, and hear my prayer . . .
I will both lie down and sleep in peace;
for you alone, O Lord, make me lie down in safety." (Ps. 4:1, 8)

The need to lament something disconcerting in life is a universal human experience. We, too, experience fear, look for escape, grow weary, and seek relief from the things that afflict us. We lament. God desires to meet us in that space, to not only come alongside us in a unique and special way, but to bring healing and comfort and a way forward. Without a doubt, in God there is strength for the journey, restoration of the soul, and hope for the righteous!

In lament, we can learn and see life from a perspective as no other. To join others in lament is to be a friend in a movement like no other. Lament is not a place to reside, but it is a place through which we all must learn to journey.

Lord Jesus, you know my fears and condition in life. Be near to your servant and answer me when I call. Provide at the level of my deepest need, restore my soul, and renew my sense of purpose in you.

Pete C. Menjares is a senior fellow with the Council for Christian Colleges & Universities and is a former pastor and university president. He currently serves as a member of the Board of Trustees at Seattle Pacific University.

Fourth Wednesday of Lent

SHARON OKAMOTO AND THE STAFF AT

SEATTLE URBAN ACADEMY

MARK 1:40–41 • COLOSSIANS 2:6–15

*A leper came to him begging him, and kneeling he said to him,
"If you choose, you can make me clean." Moved with pity, Jesus
stretched out his hand and touched him, and said to him,
"I do choose. Be made clean!"*
Mark 1:40-41

*And when you were dead in trespasses and the uncircumcision of
your flesh, God made you alive together with him, when he forgave
us all our trespasses, erasing the record that stood against us with its
legal demands. He set this aside, nailing it to the cross. He disarmed
the rulers and authorities and made a public example of them,
triumphing over them in it.*
Colossians 2:13-15

It's Never Too Late
for Resurrection

Christ Jesus—
You engage the leper.
  We cry out to you, O Christ, begging on fallen knee
  With wounds that cut deep,
  Leaving us unable to feel, to sense
  Numbness, that leads to further injury.
You move with compassion toward us,
Outstretching your hand to touch us—

Abandoned, wrenched in guilt, bound inadequate;
  Hurt by those closest to us, now closed, with inability for
intimacy;
  Abused by parents, feeling unloved, void of worth;
  Angry, depressed, self-medicated, substance-abused, suicidal.

"Are you willing? Will you make us clean?"
"I am willing. Be cleansed. Be washed free."

For in Christ, God's fullness dwells.
More than cleansed,
In Christ we have been made complete;
Not by our doing, but by Your authoritative rule.

In Christ, the wounds and secondary wounds are severed and
buried,
  Laid to rest in baptism in which we are also raised up with You
  By the powerful working of God, who raised us in Christ from
the dead.

You made us alive with You, forgiving
All that was wrong,
  that fell short of Your good,
  that was hostile to us.

"Be cleansed!" You've removed our wounds.
"I am willing!" You were nailed to the cross.

Your hand touched us, drawing us in to You,
Triumphing over death that buried our souls.

We are free, confident with joy in the worth of
Your calling
Your voice
Your word
Made flesh;

Life now in You.
Thank you, O Christ, for our resurrected life,
raised up in You.

Sharon Okamoto is the executive director and principal of Seattle Urban Academy (SUA). This devotional was written in collaboration with the staff of SUA.

Fourth Thursday of Lent

ALBERTO SOLANO

❊

PSALM 102 • MARK 3:1–6

And he said to the man who had the withered hand, "Come forward." Then he said to them, "Is it lawful to do good or to do harm on the sabbath, to save life or to kill?" But they were silent.
Mark 3:3–4

No Longer Strangers

Come forward.

Throughout the Scriptures we find many passages where Jesus healed those in pain in their bodies, in their souls, and in their relationships. In all cases Jesus acted compassionately, putting their suffering first, without giving consideration to what was politically correct and even defying traditions or the expectations of some religious professionals.

Mark described a man with a withered hand as marginalized, or impure. It could have been any person with a physical or mental disability at that time. The marginalized could not enter the synagogue; they had to wait outside or, in the best case, remain in the back. However, Jesus called this man to come forward, to stand up, and he healed him despite the presence of accusers. The man was not only healed, but called to no longer be in the margins. He was invited to move to the center—into the full presence of God and the community.

In our daily life we also can face injustice, and be witnesses of suffering and pain. Most of the time those who remain on the margins are those who suffer the most: the poor, the displaced, the migrants, those who our society, some leaders, and even our established laws have left behind. We sometimes create excuses that justify not engaging. These can seem like well-considered reasons why we should not intervene when we encounter someone in need.

What would have happened to many in the Scriptures if Jesus would have just followed the religious practices of his day? How many wouldn't have been saved, healed, or redeemed. He might have avoided conflict, accusers, or the tensions with the cultural practices of the day, but at the cost of not fulfilling his mission while on earth. We will always have the opportunity to help others. So as you read these words, be challenged to follow your heart. Follow that subtle feeling of unrest that we have learned so well to ignore. Each time it shows up, act anyway. Let's remember a cup of cold water, a kind word, or some act of kindness given in his name, is a kingdom act.

Jesus, we pray that as you call on the margins to "Come forward!" to you, grant us the grace and courage to go forward into the margins, being no longer strangers there among those for whom you show a preferential love. Amen.

Alberto Solano lives in Seattle, Washington, and is the executive director of Agros International. He and his wife, Yadira, have four children.

Fourth Friday of Lent

KEVIN FINCH

❧

JOHN 11:21 • PSALM 6

Martha said to Jesus, "Lord, if you had been here,
my brother would not have died."
John 11:21

Saying "Yes, Lord"

T. S. Eliot, in "Choruses from the Rock" says:

Endless invention, endless experiment,
Brings knowledge of motion, but not of stillness;
Knowledge of speech, but not of silence;
Knowledge of words, and ignorance of the Word.

Can we sit in silence when everything in us screams for action, for words, for a fix?

Might we, in the stillness, discover not the right words, but the Word?

I wonder if Martha wanted to take back her words to Jesus in this story? There is sharpness, an accusatory tone. She feels a betrayal in their friendship, it seems.

The wrong words often accompany lament, don't they? We say things out of pain. We say things we don't mean and we say things that may even be hurtful.

Jesus not only absorbs Martha's words, he absorbs her pain like a true friend. He also refuses the situation and speaks hope with grace.

Some of us may not be as quick to turn as Martha. But the end goal is the same: remember God is not only present; he desires and provides for resurrection.

"Yes, Lord" (John 11:27), Martha prays out loud, and invites us to join her.

Jesus, I confess that pain and tragedy and suffering scare me. I want to avoid them at all costs, and when it can't be avoided, fix it as fast as I can—for myself and for others. Would you help me show up and stay put without the need for the right words, but instead an unshakable trust that you as the Word are even more present and about your deep work of redemption?

Kevin Finch leads Big Table, a unique non-profit that cares for those in crisis in the largest industry in the nation—restaurant and hospitality.

Fourth Saturday of Lent

STEVE GARBER

❖

PSALM 22 • JOHN 11:28–44

You are my hiding place and my shield; I hope in your word.
Psalm 119:114

The Hint of Hope

Near the end of his novel, *The Moviegoer*, Walker Percy offers a meditation on the first day of Lent; not as a message for the church, but for the world—the secularizing, pluralizing, and globalizing world. Though a person of honest Christian faith, he did not write Christian stories for Christian people; he was a novelist for every man and every woman.

The New York critics even pronounced him, "the American Camus," comparing him to the French novelist/philosopher Albert Camus, whose stories wrestled in the most plaintive, poignant way with the tensions of being human in the modern world. Percy is said to have protested, "Yes, I am honest about the heartache of human life, pilgrims in the ruins that we are, but there is always a hint of hope in my writing."[9]

A hint of hope.

They are words of life for all of us in and through the Lenten season. Called as we are to more attention, more reflection, more thoughtfulness, more repentance, these are days which ask us to ask harder questions about who we are and how we live, about what we think and what we do, about the wounded world and our own wounds.

When all is said and done though, our vocation is to be hints of hope at work and at play, in our families and among our neighbors, in our cities and in our society . . . amidst the ashes of our lives and world, "pilgrims in the ruins that we are."

> *God in heaven, be merciful to us, teach us to live*
> *with hope; not because we are strong, because*
> *we are not, but because you promise to be our*
> *refuge and our shield. Hope is not optimism, so*
> *we do not believe that if we are smart enough*
> *or try hard enough that "all will be well" in this*
> *frail world; rather hope is formed by the truth of*
> *your word, which is why we hope in you. Amen.*

For many years, Steve Garber has been a teacher of many people in many places. The principal of the Washington Institute for Faith, Vocation & Culture, he is the author of *Visions of Vocation: Common Grace for the Common Good*; in addition, he serves as a fellow for the Mars Corporation and for the M. J. Murdock Charitable Trust.

Fifth Week of Lent

SUFFERING

The Taking of Christ
by Francisco de Goya (1746–1828)

Goya was a highly significant painter working in Spain during a period of enormous political upheaval in the Western world, including the American Revolution, the French Revolution, the rise and fall of the Emperor Napoleon, and the latter's invasion of Spain. To a man as observant and sensitive as Goya, all of this social violence, and the disordering impact on the social fabric, increasingly lessened his confidence in people and darkened his view of the world. His later paintings reveal an artist who is well familiar with suffering in his own life.

To notice: (1) Jesus, the beloved Son, was delivered *twice* into the hands of men: first, into the hands of Mary and Joseph his parents, where he was lovingly received, wrapped in a white cloth, and gloriously acknowledged by a gathering of all the angels of heaven (see Luke 2:1–14); second, and here, into the hands of those sent to arrest him in Gethsemane (see Luke 22:47–53), who advance chaotically with fear and weapons to seize the one still wrapped in white. (2) Over Bethlehem were arrayed the angels of heaven, who come from heaven to earth singing delight and praise; here, in Gethsemane, is arrayed an earthly host of humans, who come *not* singing—see those faces turned upward with mouths open—but shouting in rage. (3) Why is Jesus looking at that man's finger—Judas's finger—which commandingly points at the leader of the guard?

Album/Art Resource, NY

Fifth Sunday of Lent

Rick Ganz

❈

MARK 8:31–32

And he began to teach them that it was inevitable that the Son of Man should go through much suffering and be utterly repudiated by the elders and chief priests and scribes, and be killed, and after three days rise again. He told them all this quite bluntly.
Mark 8:31–32a (PHILLIPS)

Redeeming Suffering

When we consider suffering as something familiar, possibly too familiar, we may recognize how difficult it is to sort out. Is suffering the same as pain? If suffering hurts, then ought we to avoid it if we can? Is suffering just another way of describing what growing up feels like—its price? Is suffering how sacrifice feels? If suffering is a feeling, then what part of us, exactly, is feeling it? Or, if I deliberately accept suffering, then is it no longer a passion but an *action*? I think, in this latter regard, of the remarkable runner Steve Prefontaine (1951–1975), who said, "Somebody may beat me, but he is going to have to bleed to do it."

The Gospels note how explicitly Jesus said to his disciples: "He spoke this openly" (v. 32 NABRE)—and three times the Gospels tell us: "the Son of Man *must* suffer greatly and be rejected by the elders, the chief priests, and the scribes, and be killed, and rise after three days" (v. 31 NABRE, emphasis added).

That word "must" translates the Greek verb *dei*, meaning "it is [absolutely] necessary" that the Son of Man suffer greatly, be rejected, be killed . . . and rise. Such divine necessity expressed should have alerted the disciples, and us, that the Father and the Son were up to *something more* than the "suffering greatly" of the Son. We hear it in English when we say, "it is necessary, *because* . . ." Because what? Notice how the disciples did not hear "and *rise*," because understanding the purposes of the Father and Son remained outside of their capacity to receive it. As a result, they noticed the suffering, and only that—*and, therefore, misunderstood it.*

Yet this is what Jesus came to show the disciples, and us— that *something more* that he and his Father were doing, so that seeing that we might actually "not count the cost" for the sake of "laboring" (Luke 14:28) with Christ even now to show others the glorious mystery. Recall Isaiah 43:19, "See, I am doing something new! Now it springs forth, *do you not perceive it?*" (NABRE, emphasis added).

Recall an astonishing moment in the film *The Passion of the Christ* (2004), directed by Mel Gibson, an account of the final twelve hours of Jesus' life. Jesus (played by Jim Caviezel), horribly maimed by torture, and psychologically brutalized, was making his way with the cross through the city of Jerusalem. The spectacle of someone so brutalized moving among people who enjoyed gawking at the scene, counting their own good fortune or displaying their disgust at the weakness of this "criminal," is overwhelming. Jesus falls, hard, and the cross bangs down on him. Rushing up to him is Mary, his mother, who kneels down and lifts up his bloody and disfigured face toward her. What might he say to her? What *could* he say? As he looks up at her he says, "Behold, I make all things new" (Rev. 21:5 NKJV). Gibson's contemplative understanding of Jesus here is remarkable.

This is what Jesus came to show us, what he and his Father were and still are doing with this world, such that even "suffering greatly" mattered little in contrast. They were doing together a truly great thing. Saint Paul finally grasped this, which caused him in one place to exclaim: "I consider that the sufferings of this present time are *as nothing* compared with the glory to be revealed for us" (Rom. 8:18 NABRE, emphasis added).

> *Loving Father, we worry about the suffering that you state comes to those who follow you. Bless us with a greater capacity to accept our own suffering by revealing, in time, how you deepen our capacities to receive the glory that Christ gained for us.*

Rick Ganz is a member of the Society of Jesus, the Jesuits, and is the head of the Faber Institute.

Fifth Monday of Lent

JOHN ASHMEN

❖

DEUTERONOMY 2:1–8 • LUKE 8:43–48

*When the woman saw that she could not remain hidden, she came
trembling; and falling down before him, she declared in the presence
of all the people why she had touched him,
and how she had been immediately healed.*
Luke 8:47

No Silent Suffering

The compacted crowd in Luke 8 would have made a claustrophobic hyperventilate. Despite the congestion, the woman with the chronic condition wormed her way through the throng and reached her intended target: the garment of a Rabbi whose authority was to be her remedy. Instantly, he felt a discharge of power. Immediately, she felt years of hemorrhaging and hardship end.

The story of the afflicted woman is certainly one of faith and determination. But it goes deeper. Knowing what we do about her condition, and factoring in Jewish law, we likely recognize the saga of a woman who has suffered in silence, living more than a decade in a culture which considered her unclean.

In this life there will be suffering, be it related to physical pain or mental anguish. Suffering is hard enough to endure even when you have friends to fall back on, but to suffer alone amplifies the agony. We need to cast our cares on Christ, but we also need to be in community where we can seek solace and share the hurts of our heart. Ephesians 4:2 describes this as "bearing with one another in love."

I find it interesting that Jesus did not let the woman be cured incognito. He called her out from the crowd so she could tell her story. I'd like to think that she was quickly surrounded by peers with whom she could lose her cares and find her voice.

Christians should never suffer in silence—or allow others to do so.

Loving Jesus, no one understands suffering like you do. Thank you for enduring the agony of the cross and the devastation of separation from your Father, so I can embrace sacred assurances in the midst of my infirmities and grasp divine hope in the midst of my heartaches. Open my eyes to others around me who desperately need my presence and your promises in their times of suffering. Give me a deep desire to serve them selflessly. I ask this in your powerful, abiding, and comforting name, Amen.

John Ashmen is a husband, father, and grandfather, and the president of the Association of Gospel Rescue Missions (AGRM), North America's oldest and largest network of independent, faith-based crisis shelters and addiction-recovery centers.

Fifth Tuesday of Lent

LAURA GIDDINGS

PSALM 143 • LUKE 7:11–17

*Soon afterwards [Jesus] went to a town called Nain, and his disciples
and a large crowd went with him. As he approached the gate of
the town, a man who had died was being carried out. He was his
mother's only son, and she was a widow; and with her was a large
crowd from the town. When the Lord saw her, he had compassion
for her and said to her, "Do not weep." Then he came forward and
touched the bier, and the bearers stood still. And he said, "Young
man, I say to you, rise!" The dead man sat up and began to speak,
and Jesus gave him to his mother. Fear seized all of them; and they
glorified God, saying, "A great prophet has risen among us!" and
"God has looked favorably on his people!" This word about him
spread throughout Judea and all the surrounding country.*

Luke 7:11–17

Bearing Burdens

Those who study the culture of biblical times tell us that a
woman who lost her spouse and had no son to support her
became either dependent on relatives or consigned to suffer a
lonely existence on the margins of society. Jesus understood the
widow's grief through his own human experience of death, as we
know through the story of Lazarus. But as someone concerned
with everyone on the margins of society, Jesus also understood
the implications for the widow's life. He had compassion for her
in her moment of grief, as well as for her lonely future.

Jean Vanier, the founder of L'Arche, wrote in *Becoming Human*,
"To be lonely is to feel unwanted and unloved, and therefore

unlovable. Loneliness is a taste of death." By bringing the widow's son back to life, Jesus also gave the widow back her life.

Few of us will have the chance to bring someone back to life from physical death. However, we all carry within us the capacity to do miracles too. Any one of us, on any day, can banish the emotional death of loneliness by reaching out with compassion to make an authentic connection with another person. In L'Arche, we call this miracle mutual relationship, and it is our mission. Through countless daily acts of care, we strive to give comfort as Jesus did. In doing so, we find our life together in community.

Loneliness is perhaps one of the modern world's greatest sadness. How much pain is caused by those reaching out in desperation of love, attention, or connection? We are Christ's ambassadors when we reach out and touch those in need. Who is that person God has placed in your path this day?

Lord, help us to remember that we, too, can work miracles in one another's lives. Fill us with your compassion, so that we may be a source of comfort and life to those who are suffering from grief and loneliness. Amen.

Laura Giddings is the executive director and community leader of L'Arche Tahoma Hope in Tacoma, Washington, which is 1 of 148 member communities of the International Federation of L'Arche.

Fifth Wednesday of Lent

Lawrence Ho

JOSHUA 7:1–10 • 1 CORINTHIANS 10:13

No testing has overtaken you that is not common to everyone.
God is faithful, and he will not let you be tested beyond your strength,
but with the testing he will also provide the way out
so that you may be able to endure it.
1 Corinthians 10:13

The Privilege
of Suffering

The apostle Paul's letters to the Romans and Corinthians allow our sufferings to be seen in the light of God's scandalous gift of grace. As followers of Jesus, we are called to be content in much and in little (see Philippians 4:11–13). This must also include our approach to suffering, difficulties, and trials. How much faith or grace is required when all is going well? Can we find ways to rejoice and understand our sufferings and trials in light of how it produces "perseverance, character, and ultimately hope" (see Romans 5:3–4)? That is the hope and promise of glory both for this earth and the next.

If we say that it is not fair that we suffer for Adam's sin and within a fallen world, then it must also be unfair that we are redeemed by Jesus' righteous death at the cross. Jesus took on all the sins of history—past, present, and future—so that we could become righteousness covered by the blood of the Lamb. This is the divine transaction and the necessity of Jesus' birth, death, and resurrection in glory.

Sufferings become our opportunity to participate in the following of Christ as the Last Adam. And he also promises not to give us more than we can bear (see 1 Corinthians 10:13). The privilege of such suffering is the true meaning of this season of Lent. Suffering draws us closer to Jesus' suffering and, ultimately, to our Heavenly Father's rescue plan for humankind.

And where there is suffering, trials, and difficulty, there is all the more room for God's grace to abound (see Romans 5:20–21), both for speaking into our lives personally, and as a testimony to those around us. All this, for the glory of his name and his "kingdom come . . . on earth as it is in heaven" (Matt. 6:10).

> *Lord have mercy; Christ have mercy.*
> *Dear Heavenly Father, in our suffering, brokenness,*
> *and trials, would you be glorified? Remind us*
> *that we are a work in progress, and that we'll*
> *only be perfected with your mysterious refining*
> *purposes. Thank you being there for us and for not*
> *allowing us to suffer beyond what we can bear.*

Lawrence Ho serves as a senior fellow to the M. J. Murdock Charitable Trust. Lawrence is an attorney, primarily advising families in their philanthropy. Along with his wife, Dr. Angela Lee, they own and operate a medical clinic in Vancouver, British Columbia, Canada.

Fifth Thursday of Lent

Felix Rosales

❧

MARK 9:14–29 • ACTS 7:54–60

*Someone from the crowd answered him, "Teacher, I brought you my
son; he has a spirit that makes him unable to speak . . ."*
Mark 9:17

Freedom to
the Captive

Why is there so much suffering in the world? Why does God
not miraculously stop it? These questions are difficult to answer,
especially when we experience suffering ourselves, or when a
family member or friend is suffering.

In this passage from Mark 9, we see one example of human
suffering. We learn about a distraught father who had used
every means at his disposal to free his suffering son from being
possessed by a destructive spirit.

Unable to find someone to help him, the father approached the
disciples of Jesus Christ, hoping they could release his son. But
they could not do it. The man then went to Jesus Christ, who
immediately perceives the root of this suffering and exclaims: "O
faithless generation" (Mark 9:19 NABRE). Seems like something

Jesus might say today; in fact, to every generation! We are slow to learn that believing in Jesus Christ is the way to find deliverance. He immediately orders the destructive spirit to leave the boy, and then Jesus heals him completely. Though not every story turns out this way, it does remind us that freedom is God's ultimate desire for all of us. Sometimes it comes fast, sometimes slow, and sometimes not as we expect.

In his mission as Savior and Lord, Jesus Christ became human to give his life as a ransom for many. He experienced in his own body the cruelest suffering when he was nailed to a cross, dying a criminal's death, even though he was without sin. He took on the sin of the world, so those who believe in him would receive forgiveness and salvation. Sin remains the root of suffering in the world, but Jesus Christ is always the answer to suffering. Hopefully we can be a generation who believes in Jesus Christ and the power of his resurrection. Every time we work to see suffering relieved, we are agents of Jesus.

God of all power and great love, I pray right now
for those who may be experiencing suffering.
May they receive the help they are seeking by
your healing power, and through your servants,
in the name of our Lord Jesus Christ.

Felix Rosales was born in Nicaragua, and is the president of Hispanic Ministries, based in Vancouver, Washington. Felix and his wife, Edith, have been married for thirty-seven years, and have two sons and three grandchildren.

Fifth Friday of Lent

STEPHANIE AHN MATHIS

PSALM 63 • JOHN 16:16–24

O God, you are my God, I seek you, my soul thirsts for you; my flesh faints for you, as in a dry and weary land where there is no water.
Psalm 63:1

When Suffering Yells for Hope

It is hard to hope because we risk the chance that our hope will be disappointed.

The Shunammite woman of 2 Kings 4 longed to have a child. To birth new life from barrenness. To be a cocreator with the Creator. And like Mary and Elizabeth, a miraculous birth occurred to a childless woman in old age. This hope was then crushed as she witnesses a violent, unexpected death of her young son, just as later it was the same for Mary and Elizabeth. All of these women experienced the high hopes of new life and then the deep despair of death.

I know what it is to long for a child, to love that child, and to have suffered the loss of two pregnancies. I don't want to hope because I don't want hope to be crushed. Suffering stinks.

Suffering points to the brokenness in our lives, relationships, systems, and creation. Suffering longs for better and cries for help in our fragile humanness. Suffering shouts, "Hosanna! Save us!" Suffering yells for hope. Romans 5:3–4 says that suffering is what gives birth to hope with character and perseverance. Without suffering, hope is not meaningful. It is the resurrection without the crucifixion.

Therefore, let us not move too quickly from Good Friday to Easter Sunday, but allow our suffering, the suffering of Christ, and the suffering of the world to sink into the longings of our souls. May we let ourselves thirst in the dryness of this barren land for new life and let the suffering birth hope that is now and eternal.

Jesus, thank you that you are always near to the brokenhearted and suffering. Give us the faith in areas we doubt, hope in our depressing despair, and love in place of our deepest fears. O God, may we earnestly seek you in our barrenness and thirst.

Stephanie Ahn Mathis serves as copastor with her husband, Mark, at West Hills Covenant Church. They have a son, Noah, and another child soon to arrive. Stephanie has an open, professing, foolish addiction to hope.

Fifth Saturday of Lent

Bob Kuhn

❖

LUKE 6:20–23 • 2 CORINTHIANS 4:7–18

So we do not lose heart. Even though our outer nature is wasting away, our inner nature is being renewed day by day. For this slight momentary affliction is preparing us for an eternal weight of glory beyond all measure . . .
2 Corinthians 4:16–17

The Weight of Glory

The disease crept through my body, taking over one limb at a time. Muscles cramped and the tremors eliminated the ability to thread a needle, shave with a blade or, sometimes, even to get a spoonful of soup to my mouth.

Diagnosed in January 2006, Parkinson's disease now had me firmly in its ever-tightening grip and I could not escape. "Why, Lord?" I asked as I observe the health of others and their care-free laughter. This could not be what God intended. How could I serve my God in the way that I had planned? This incessant crippling squeezed my courage and my confidence until I cringed in fear. "Do not lose heart!" It is as if the voice of the apostle Paul, warm but strong, speaks encouragement to me, as he did to the Corinthians (2 Cor. 4:16–17). It is for good you have been chosen to endure.

And in these darkest days when panic pierces to the heart, our Lord gives encouragement. The suffering Christ gives us his light of hope to shine in our hearts; his power to enable our fragile human frames to give him glory. Our weakness, his strength; our failings, his victory; our transitory lives, his eternal presence. Trusting, I let go and know that as I share the smallest sip of suffering, he has given a calling unimagined until now. And I begin to see, though dimly, his great purpose in it all.

Dear Jesus, Lord, who knew the pain was meant for me, for good, who shares my cup so I could say that it's because of you that I have something to give. In the name of Christ who bears it all because he loves us all.

Bob Kuhn is a lawyer by training, but is currently serving as the president of Trinity Western University, from which he graduated in 1972, and at which he met his wife. He speaks and writes on living positively with Parkinson's disease.

The Tree of Life

Every tree has a story to tell,
of wind and rain and sunny days,
of birds who found a place to sing their song.
They speak of snowy days with limbs weighed down,
And summer heat and roots sunk deep.

Some think the growth of trees is happenstance,
an accident if windblown seed or perfect place.
But wisdom whispers that fruitfulness
comes not by chance, but careful care
weaved skillfully of painful prune and willful trim,
of elements and time.

The sun's true pull brings
life to life!
And trees grow to give and live and
bear the fruit of their promise
as a seed.

Holy Week

THE DEATH
OF JESUS

The Deposition
by Jacopo Robusti "Tintoretto" (1518–1594)

Tintoretto, a nickname—"little dyer"—given him as the eldest son of a master dyer, was a late Renaissance painter of the Venetian school, who, like El Greco, was for a time a student of Titian. The latter rejected him as his pupil after only a couple of weeks, because he saw that the boy was prodigiously gifted but unteachably independent of mind. One particularly interesting commitment of his was to make a painting with full awareness ahead of time as to exactly where it would be hung on a wall, so that he could paint the perspectives in relation to those coming to look at his paintings. This reflects Tintoretto's concern to make his painting respond to its intended location.[10]

To notice: (1) It appears that *two* people have died at the cross, not only Jesus but also his mother, who lie in relation to each other in the form of a cross. Notice a contrast with the earlier Michelangelo's *Pieta*: Mary, strong but sorrowing, fully supports her son in her lap and arms; Tintoretto follows Michelangelo's design—Jesus in the lap of his mother—but dramatically reinterprets this moment at the cross. (2) Tintoretto places the woman, with arms outstretched, who looks closely into the shadowed face of Jesus, in the central position in his painting. The way her arms extend like wings, and hers the only face not marked by shadow, gives the strong impression of an angel sent to check on Jesus. (3) In the bottom right of the painting we see the hammer by which nails are driven in, and tongs by which they are extracted—a vivid symbol of our uncomfortable relation to God who scares us: our desire to control him (the hammer that holds Christ in place) and the desire to let God do as God wishes (the tongs releasing our nails).

Cameraphoto Arte, Venice/Art Resource, NY

Palm Sunday

RICK GANZ

❖

JOHN 19:38–42

After this, Joseph of Arimathea, secretly a disciple of Jesus for fear of the Jews, asked Pilate if he could remove the body of Jesus. And Pilate permitted it. So he came and took his body. Nicodemus, the one who had first come to him at night, also came bringing a mixture of myrrh and aloes weighing about one hundred pounds.
John 19:38–39 (NABRE)

Truth's Superb Surprise

Emily Dickinson expressed in a poem an insight that we need when speaking to the death of Jesus, laboring to express a meaning that lies deeper than what words can possibly capture. She wrote:

Tell all the truth but tell it slant—
Success in Circuit lies
Too bright for our infirm Delight
The Truth's superb surprise
As Lightning to the Children eased
With explanation kind
The Truth must dazzle gradually
Or every man be blind—[11]

Might we consider that we "tell it slant"—the story of Jesus' Passion and dying and death—when we concentrate on Jesus' death: how he died, step by agonizing step; the intense physical evocations of his physical sufferings in our imagination; noticing those who were most actively effecting his murder, who failed him, and so forth? I am suggesting that we are choosing to speak *along* the truth ("slant"), rather than right at it, when we allow our religious attention to affix itself upon his suffering and death, and then imagine that we are honoring him by doing so. We, in a certain way, habitually avoid paying attention to *that which was most important to Jesus* about his Passion and death. What was important to Jesus was *not* his death . . . and so why should it be so for us?

What *was* important to Jesus was his life among us, the unconquerable life of the beloved Son, whose love and purposes were vastly stronger than his death on the cross. The Old Testament already knew that Love was *as strong as* death:

> *Set me as a seal upon your heart,*
> *as a seal upon your arm;*
> *For Love is strong as Death,*
> *longing is fierce as Sheol.*
> *Its arrows are arrows of fire,*
> *flames of the divine.*
> *Deep waters cannot quench love,*
> *nor rivers sweep it away.*
> *Were one to offer all the wealth of his house for love,*
> *he would be utterly despised.* (Song of Solomon 8:6–7 NABRE)

However, Jesus raised from the dead proved that *divine love was stronger* than death. Peter confidently asserted this in his speech in Jerusalem at Pentecost: "But God raised him up, releasing him from the throes of death, because it was *impossible* for him to be held by it" (Acts 2:24 NABRE, emphasis added).

So if Jesus knows the sure and certain love of his Father for him, the beloved Son, and has already understood that the Father would raise him up through death on the third day—three times he announced this fact to his disciples—then why have Christians so often paid far more attention to the dying and death of Jesus than to his resurrection and ascension . . . and how these mysteries turn death on its head? "Behold, I make all things new" (Rev. 21:5 NABRE).

Could it be that Christians remain preoccupied with the conviction that death is the enemy, when the Father has proven that it no longer is? Could it be that the Spirit is unable to teach us about this because we won't let God teach us? Yet if we did finally grasp this good news, then how much of what we are worried about in our daily lives would lose its fundamental source in our intractable[12] conviction that death still wins in the end?

What would the Passion and death of Jesus become for us in our contemplation of it this year if we perceived it through the unconquerable love and faith of Jesus, the inner fierceness in him rooted in the faithfulness of his Father. "Now faith means putting *our full confidence* in the things we hope for, it means *being certain* of things we cannot see" (Heb. 11:1 PHILLIPS, emphasis mine).

Jesus, grant us the capacity to become preoccupied
with the fierceness of spirit that you felt, and
the opportunity given you to express to your
Father the untamed love for and faith in him
that you had and so majestically proved.

Rick Ganz is a member of the Society of Jesus, the Jesuits, and is the head of the Faber Institute.

Monday of Holy Week

SHELDON NORD

ISAIAH 53:1–3 • MARK 14:1–20

My servant grew up in the LORD's presence like a tender green shoot,
like a root in dry ground.
There was nothing beautiful or majestic about his appearance,
nothing to attract us to him.
He was despised and rejected—
a man of sorrows, acquainted with deepest grief.
We turned our backs on him and looked the other way.
He was despised, and we did not care.
Isaiah 53:2–3 (NLT)

Reframing Our Focus

"Despised and rejected." These are not words with which I want to become intimate. They are uncomfortable to me, to mankind. We humans are not drawn to the negative. Consider the following pairs of words and see which column you gravitate toward:

Winning	Losing
First	Last
Receiving	Sacrificing
Beautiful	Unattractive
Applauded	Rejected
Joy	Sorrow

The words on the left pull on us like magnets. We want to live in their presence because they are our comfort zone.

How our flesh cringes at those words on the right. They bring us down, discourage us. But it's those words, as we see in our reading for today that describe Jesus Christ, our Savior.

How do we resolve the dissonance we feel about this! Our flesh cries out for the attractive, the things that our culture praises. But our spirits quiet within, pause and ponder: If the gospel (God made flesh in Christ) dwells in the undesirable, how might I change my posture to be more receptive to him there?

What if the answer is not in radically shunning all things worldly or glamorous and beautiful, but rather in learning how to embrace the full spectrum of life? What if we could learn to sit, and sit well, with people and circumstances that fall on opposite ends of the spectrum and anything in between—from royalty to poverty, from all to nothing, and from life to death? Because somehow, in the messiness and ugliness we try so hard to avoid, we find Jesus.

Lord Jesus, forgive me for avoiding the things and people in this world that cause me discomfort. I want to begin seeing you in every circumstance and in every person around me, and in so doing somehow become more like you. You are worthy of all praise, and I rejoice that yours is the kingdom and the glory forever and ever. Amen.

Sheldon Nord is the president of Corban University in Salem, Oregon. He and his beautiful wife, Jamie, have been married twenty-eight years and they have one daughter, Hannah.

Tuesday of Holy Week

A. J. Swoboda

❖

ISAIAH 53:4–6 • MARK 14:22–41

*But he was wounded for our transgressions, crushed for our
iniquities; upon him was the punishment that made us whole,
and by his bruises we are healed.*
Isaiah 53:5

The Healing Power of Wounds

Isaiah peers into his future, describing a time of healing when forgiveness and justice and mercy would reconcile God's people back to God. "All we," writes Isaiah, "have gone astray" (53:6a). The prophet's message still has bite: everyone is guilty. But consider the verse's finale. The "iniquity of us all" has been laid upon him (53:6b). With lucid clarity, Old Testament scholar Derek Kidner points out the significance of the Hebrew word play in the verse's first and last words. Kidner concludes, "the expressions, all we . . . we all, which give the verse an identical beginning and end in Hebrew; grace wholly answering sin."

"We all" are broken, and "we all" are healed. How does this healing take place? Isaiah doesn't mince words: "by his bruises we are healed" (53:5).

Almost immediately following his resurrection, Jesus returns to his disciples. His appearances include eating meals and walking through walls. But one mustn't ignore his appearance to Thomas—that "doubting" disciple. There, Jesus shows Thomas his scars.

Theologically, it isn't inconsequential to recognize that Jesus very well could have been resurrected scarless. Resurrection could have meant a pristine, mark-free body. But resurrection doesn't hide death. Jesus had scars. And the impact of those was anything short of miraculous. The doubter became missionary. Tradition long suggests Thomas went to India following his radical encounter with the living Christ and being invited to feel those scars firsthand.

This Lent season, let us be reminded of Henri Nouwen's book *The Wounded Healer.* Jesus is the greatest healer because, from his woundedness, he healed and set healing in motion in you and me. He chose to minister out of his woundedness and to make that a part of the fullness of who he is. And we are the same. We bring healing not by ignoring our wounds, but by embracing them. Like him, we minister out of our scars, not our perfections.

Lord, we touch your wounds today. And by doing so, would you heal us, send us and revive us? O God, may your wounds heal us, set us free, and make us agents of your healing wholeness.

A. J. Swoboda pastors Theophilus Church in Portland, Oregon, and is the executive director of the Stewardship Alliance of the nonprofit Blessed Earth.

Wednesday of Holy Week

JAN MUSGROVE ELFERS

❧

ISAIAH 53:7–9 • MARK 15:6–40

By a perversion of justice he was taken away. Who could have imagined his future? For he was cut off from the land of the living, stricken for the transgression of my people.
Isaiah 53:8

Embracing Brokenness

On a pristine, bluebird-sky day in Hawaii, while she was enjoying a long-anticipated family vacation with her husband, children, and grandchildren, my mother died unexpectedly as we were snorkeling off the coast of Lanai. In the days and months after her death, my grief brought up questions about the nature of suffering. Like Jesus, we may feel abandoned by God in our darkest hours. We may think that we are being punished by God. Or we may feel angry or undeserving of the pain we are experiencing.

The reality is that suffering is an inevitable part of being human. In Jesus, we are given a model for human suffering and a way into hope. Jesus suffered without being defensive or seeking violence or retribution. Yet he honestly wrestled with feelings of despair. In Jesus, we are given an example of how we can go to God in our pain, secure in the knowledge that we can bring our whole selves to him, even our doubts and fears.

God is intimately with us always, especially in the midst of our suffering. When surrendered, suffering can transform us into Christ's likeness. Then our pain enables us to be more fully present, in grace, tenderness, and humility, to the suffering of the people close to us and to the world beyond us. We can confidently go to God in prayer because we know that Jesus suffered all things, so he might be able to be present to us in all things.

*Loving God, may we bring our whole selves
to you, even in our darkest hours, knowing
that since Jesus suffered all things, he is able to
understand and be near to us in our suffering.*

Jan Musgrove Elfers is the executive director of Ecumenical Ministries of Oregon. Jan and her husband, Michael, have two children and she is a third generation Oregonian.

Maundy Thursday

TARA RUSSELL

❊

ISAIAH 53:10–12 • JOHN 19:1–15

Still, it's what GOD had in mind all along,
to crush him with pain.
The plan was that he give himself as an offering for sin
so that he'd see life come from it—life, life, and more life.
And GOD's plan will deeply prosper through him.
Out of that terrible travail of soul,
he'll see that it's worth it and be glad he did it.
Through what he experienced, my righteous one, my servant,
will make many "righteous ones,"
as he himself carries the burden of their sins.
Therefore I'll reward him extravagantly—
the best of everything, the highest honors—
Because he looked death in the face and didn't flinch,
because he embraced the company of the lowest.
He took on his own shoulders the sin of the many,
he took up the cause of all the black sheep.
Isaiah 53:10–12 (MSG)

The Strength for Today

Life is complex, and often full of significant challenges. When
we remain focused inwardly on our own pain and every difficulty we face, it can at times feel suffocating and seemingly
insurmountable. Having just come through a few of the most
challenging years of my life, along with a recent nasty flu bug,
I was reminded how debilitating it can be to focus on our own
challenges.

When I look at the life of Jesus from afar, it seems outlandish that he would suffer such tragic pain and so much intentional harm—all for our good. He knew what was coming his way, and yet I imagine he daily gained courage by remaining others focused and knowing clearly his mission and purpose, far beyond himself.

In my own life, when I am able to maintain an others-focused view of the world, I am less concerned about the issues I face or feel daily. I find myself preoccupied with caring for the needs of others, working to serve and support realities far beyond just myself. This is the place I am most effective as a leader and most satisfied. And yet it requires a disciplined daily focus on God—a reminder of the life and death of Jesus—and strength and stamina for each day ahead.

Jesus, I'm grateful to know you intimately— your strength and your suffering. Empower me with your courage and others focus, and when I'm weak or get derailed, please bring me the strength to get back my focus.

Tara Russell is a social entrepreneur based in Boise, Idaho, with her husband, Jeff, and two kids, Tyson and Lucy. Tara serves as founder and president of Fathom, along with a variety of other social enterprises she has cofounded over the past twenty years.

Good Friday

MARSHALL SNIDER

❧

JOHN 19:17–28 • ISAIAH 55:1–5

After this, when Jesus knew that all was now finished, he said (in order to fulfill the scripture), "I am thirsty."
John 19:28

Begin with the End in Mind

Jesus did not cut corners. He didn't take a drink until he knew it was all finished. He knew what needed to be done and he accomplished it.

How many of us have started something and not finished what we started? What were the implications, the penalties, and the repercussions of this? Christ's work was thorough, it was complete; he did not skip steps. Each step he fully executed, because each was important for the work of reconciling man to God. The work had to be complete and in fulfillment of the scripture.

I believe that Christ began with the end in mind. It was the end which helped him as he suffered—the salvation of you and me, for example. He saw us in darkness alienated from the presence of the Father because of our desire to go our own way, our searching and seeking for truth and understanding. He saw the pain before he felt it; he saw the nails in the hands before his were nailed to the cross. All of this he saw before he began the process of his death. He had to have seen and understood this ahead of time, so that he could know when the work was fully accomplished. Only then did he ask for relief from his thirst; only then did he say, "It is finished" (John 19:30). Thank you, Jesus, for your finished work.

> *Thank you, Jesus, for your finished work. Thank you for not cutting corners and for spending yourself on us. We are so grateful for your work. May your example of work fully accomplished inspire us to finish our work as well, the work you have laid out for each of us. May we be able, then, to say, "It is finished!" Amen.*

Marshall Snider is the founder and executive director of Because People Matter (BridgeTown Inc.), an urban humanitarian work focusing on creating relational environments that create mobilization, relief, and transformation in Portland, Oregon. He has been married to Lesley for twenty-three years, has two sons, and resides in Canby, Oregon.

Holy Saturday

MAUREEN FIFE

❀

MATTHEW 27:45–50 • ISAIAH 55:6–9

Then Jesus cried again with a loud voice and breathed his last.
Matthew 27:50

A Restless Discomfort

How could we help but feel unequal to grasping the depth and gift of the last powerful hours of Christ on this earth?

Christ took the sins of man upon himself and freely sacrificed his life in accordance with the scripture. I cannot imagine enduring the emotional, physical, and spiritual pain of his hours on the cross. In the last moments of Christ's agonizing hours as a man on the earth, he reveals his humanity when he cries out, "My God, my God, why have you forsaken me?" (Matt. 27:46). He shares with us his deepest moments of utter despair.

Then, Jesus cried out a second time, giving up his spirit to God the Father, with the offering of his life for ours fully accomplished.

Jesus paid the ultimate price for our eternal salvation, and we are compelled to honor that sacrifice. I believe we are called to be the hands and feet of Christ, sharing our human compassion, empathy, love, and faith through a life of service.

A Benedictine Sister, Ruth Fox once prayed:

May God bless you with a restless discomfort about easy answers, half-truths and superficial relationships, so that you may seek truth boldly and love deep within your heart.

May God bless you with holy anger at injustice, oppression, and exploitation of people, so that you may tirelessly work for justice, freedom, and peace among all people.

May God bless you with the gift of tears to shed with those who suffer from pain, rejection, starvation, or the loss of all that they cherish so that you may reach out your hand to comfort them and transform their pain into joy.

May God bless you with enough foolishness to believe that you really can make a difference in this world, so that you are able, with God's grace, to do what others claim cannot be done.[13]

God desires to have our hearts break his heart. He also desires for his kingdom to come and his will be done by you and I on earth—as it is in heaven.

Maureen Fife has served as CEO of Tacoma/Pierce County Habitat for Humanity, a Christian housing ministry, since 2006. Through partnerships with local congregations and volunteers her affiliate has built more than two hundred fifty homes. Maureen and her husband, Mark, reside in Gig Harbor, Washington.

Easter Week

THE RESURRECTION
OF JESUS

Resurrection of the Christ
by Peter Paul Rubens (1577–1640)

In the seventeenth century in northern Europe, no artist dominated that artistic scene more than this Flemish painter, humanist, draughtsman, and diplomat, who was the other great artistic innovator of this period with Caravaggio. Peter Paul Rubens commanded a profound knowledge of Classical art and literature, trained with painters in Italy during the High Renaissance, and became a master painter in Antwerp's Guild of St. Luke by age twenty-one. He mastered Latin (a product of his Catholic school education in Antwerp), as well as Dutch, Italian, and French, and executed works in paint, sculpture, metalwork, decorations, and tapestries. He was also a skilled teacher who drew pupils from all over Europe and was the most influential teacher of Anthony van Dyck (see Week 4).[14]

To notice: Perhaps we imagine that Jesus had accomplished his divine mission in this world (cf. John 19:30) when he had breathed his last on the cross and died. And so we might consider the resurrection to be a kind of *reward* given him by the Father, and a proof to us all that God had turned aside sin's most fearsome weapon—death; i.e., death as void. This might then cause us to imagine that the Christ should come from his tomb in majestic stillness and with no work left to do. Rubens's insight startles us when he paints the Christ literally exploding from the tomb, filled with focused forcefulness—a wounded fierceness—and obviously more dangerous than ever against the world's darkness. It is as if Rubens's senses that the really great work of the Christ has only now just begun.

Bridgeman-Giraudon/Art Resource, NY

Easter Sunday

Bob Sanders

JOHN 20:1–9 • 1 CORINTHIANS 15:3–8, 12–26, 55–58

*For what I received I passed on to you as of first importance:
that Christ died for our sins according to the Scriptures,
that he was buried, that he was raised on the third day
according to the Scriptures, and that he appeared to Cephas,
and then to the Twelve. After that, he appeared to more than
five hundred of the brothers and sisters at the same time,
most of whom are still living, though some have fallen asleep.
Then he appeared to James, then to all the apostles, and last
of all he appeared to me also, as to one abnormally born.*
1 Corinthians 15:3–8 (NIV)

*Early on the first day of the week, while it was still dark,
Mary Magdalene went to the tomb and saw that the stone had
been removed from the entrance. So she came running to
Simon Peter and the other disciple, the one Jesus loved, and said,
"They have taken the Lord out of the tomb, and we don't know
where they have put him!" So Peter and the other disciple started
for the tomb. Both were running, but the other disciple outran
Peter and reached the tomb first. He bent over and looked in at
the strips of linen lying there but did not go in. Then Simon Peter
came along behind him and went straight into the tomb.
He saw the strips of linen lying there, as well as the cloth that
had been wrapped around Jesus' head. The cloth was still lying in
its place, separate from the linen. Finally the other disciple, who
had reached the tomb first, also went inside. He saw and believed.*
John 20:1–8 (NIV)

What Easter Means

What does Easter mean?

It's more than blooming flowers or chocolate eggs or the fertility of bunnies. Easter is about resurrection—our Lord's and ours. In 1 Corinthians 15, Paul promises that just as Christ is raised from the dead so shall we be raised from death.

"If Christ has not been raised," Paul insists, "our preaching is useless and so is your faith. . . . If only for this life we have hope in Christ, we are of all people most to be pitied" (1 Cor. 15:14, 19 NIV).

What does Easter mean? It means we don't have to go on living in death's dark shadow. Death is a powerful enemy—the "last enemy," (v. 26 NIV) is how Paul puts it. But on Easter, our Lord defeated this last enemy and liberated us from death's terror. So the American evangelist Dwight Moody said near the end of his life, "One day you will hear that I am dead. Do not believe it. I will then be alive as never before."[15] So Dietrich Bonhoeffer said to a friend when the Nazi guards came to take him to the gallows, "This is the end, but for me it is the beginning of life."[16]

The beginning of life—that's what Easter means. What does it feel like? We get a preview in J. R. R. Tolkien's book *The Return of the King*. If you read it or saw the movie, you know it tells the tale of a final, decisive battle between the forces of good and evil. Afterward, two of the heroes, Samwise Gamgee and Gandalf the Wizard, unexpectedly find each other alive. Sam says,

> "Gandalf! I thought you were dead! But then I thought I
> was dead myself. Is everything sad going to come untrue?
> What's happened to the world?"
>
> "A great Shadow has departed," said Gandalf, and then
> he laughed, and the sound was like music, or like water
> in a parched land; and as he listened the thought came
> to Sam that he had not heard laughter, the pure sound
> of merriment, for days upon days without count. It fell
> upon his ears like the echo of all the joys he had ever
> known. But he himself burst into tears. Then, as a sweet

rain will pass down a wind of spring and the sun will shine out the clearer, his tears ceased, and his laughter welled up, and laughing he sprang from his bed.

"How do I feel?" he cried. "Well, I don't know how to say it. I feel, I feel"—he waved his arms in the air—"I feel like spring after winter, and sun on the leaves; and like trumpets and harps and all the songs I have ever heard!"[17]

Music and springtime and laughter—that's what Easter means. The great Shadow has departed and now everything sad comes untrue. For at that great battle on Golgotha our ancient enemy was defeated. When Jesus rose from the grave, death's power to destroy us was forever broken.

"Where, O death is your victory? Where, O death, is your sting? The sting of death is sin, and the power of sin is the law. But thanks be to God, who gives us the victory through our Lord Jesus Christ" (1 Cor. 15:55–57 NIV).

He is risen! He is risen indeed! That's what Easter means.

Oh gracious and loving God, we thank you for meeting and walking with us on this journey to the cross and now walking with us from the empty tomb and into the world of our lives. May we walk from this day and practice resurrection in the days and moments of our lives.

Bob Sanders and his wife, Debbie, live in Lake Oswego, Oregon. He served Lake Grove Presbyterian Church for twenty-four years as senior pastor and now advises and encourages leaders.

Monday of Eastertide

KATHERINE GOTTLIEB

❊

MATTHEW 28:1–10 • DANIEL 7:9

*After the sabbath, as the first day of the week was dawning, Mary
Magdalene and the other Mary went to see the tomb. And suddenly
there was a great earthquake; for an angel of the Lord, descending
from heaven, came and rolled back the stone and sat on it. His
appearance was like lightning, and his clothing white as snow. For
fear of him the guards shook and became like dead men. But the
angel said to the women, "Do not be afraid; I know that you are
looking for Jesus who was crucified. He is not here; for he has been
raised, as he said. Come, see the place where he lay."*
Matthew 28:1–6

Clearing Blocked Hearts

We read God's Word, having read them before; looking at
them for wisdom and listening to him speak. And sometimes
we breeze through his Word as we do so many times reading
any other book we pick up.

And as I read these words, and talked them over with my
brother, we asked one another: Are there people who have a large
stone blocking their hearts from this awesome truth? Jesus is
alive. He is not dead; he rose as he promised from death to life.

So many today are like the Pharisees who still don't believe in
the resurrection of Jesus Christ. We still guard our hearts like
the stone in front of the tomb. We make sure nothing will steal
the lies we believe. For many of us, our hearts are blocked.

Do we have a stone that needs to be rolled away from our hearts, blocking truth? Is there some fear when we hear his words of truth? Do we need a violent earthquake to roll the stone away and an angel to tell us not to fear?

In the Bible, the book we may sometimes just breeze through, it tells us truth over and over again and again in so many different ways and so many passages. Christ died and he was raised from the dead; he has risen!

May God unblock our hearts and roll the stone away. Our pathway to heaven is told through this story. God said we must die, but he made a way for us to be with him throughout eternity. Jesus died, paid the price for our sins. Then he rose from that death. He rose from the dead, and so shall we! Is something blocking the truth from our hearts? Let's pray that God will roll away the stone or fear. He has risen and risen indeed! He has risen and he will come again to receive us unto himself.

Katherine Gottlieb is a Christian, wife of Kevin Gottlieb, mother of six, grandmother of twenty-eight, great-grandmother of five, and is of Filipino and Supiaq (Alaska Native) descent. Katherine is the CEO of Southcentral Foundation, a pilot, a MacArthur awardee, and a champion of family wellness in the Alaska Native community.

Tuesday of Eastertide

JIM CARLSON

❖

MARK 16:1–12 • ROMANS 8:12–17

*So they went out and fled from the tomb, for terror and amazement
had seized them; and they said nothing to anyone,
for they were afraid.*
Mark 16:8

We Are His Hands
and Feet

In the earliest copies of the Gospel of Mark that are available
to us, the book ends with Mark 16:8, "So they went out and fled
from the tomb, for terror and amazement had seized them; and
they said nothing to anyone, for they were afraid."

This is an admittedly awkward way to end Mark's gospel
account because, in contrast to the other three, Mark's contains
no happy account of an appearance of Jesus. We can understand why those who had copied the New Testament from its
earliest versions were tempted to add or "fill in the blank" in the
narrative, leaving the church with a longer, happier ending as a
well-intentioned epilogue to the gospel.

So, Mark's abruptness notwithstanding, where are we to find
the body of the resurrected Jesus? Scripture is clear that the

glorified body of the Christ has ascended to reign at the right hand of the Father. Is he, then, nowhere to be seen? Are we, like our sisters that first Easter morning, left with a combination of fear, trembling, and wondering?

Not hardly.

By the provision of the Spirit of Christ, God's people, the church, came together to form the representative body of Christ. Romans 8:14 declares that those whom the indwelling Spirit animates and leads, these are Christ's current representatives on earth—we are his hands and feet! And the Spirit does not countenance fear, but rather brings the joy of divine adoption and victory (see Romans 8:15–17).

While fear and uncertainty may occasionally plague us in this life, the story of God being present in the world is still being written—in a unique way through you and me. May the story we write be one that makes clear that he came to give life—and give it abundantly!

Gracious God, giver of a great cloud of witnesses and a worldwide community of brothers and sisters in Christ, may we by our love of those around us bear witness to the hope and wholeness all may find in you.

Jim Carlson is president of Montana Bible College in Bozeman, Montana. He and his wife, Mary, have served the town-and-country culture of "Big Sky Country" for more than thirty-five years.

Wednesday of Eastertide

ANDREA SCOFIELD

❖

LUKE 24:1–12 • 1 CORINTHIANS 15:1–11

Now I would remind you, brothers and sisters, of the good news that I proclaimed to you, which you in turn received, in which also you stand, through which also you are being saved, if you hold firmly to the message that I proclaimed to you—unless you have come to believe in vain.
For I handed on to you as of first importance what I in turn had received: that Christ died for our sins in accordance with the scriptures, and that he was buried, and that he was raised on the third day in accordance with the scriptures.
1 Corinthians 15:1–4

The Whole Truth, and Nothing but the Truth

Working outdoors allows me the privilege of spending time in God's creation. It strikes me that trees never have to be told how to be trees and birds know how to be birds. We human beings, however, need reminding how to be ourselves—people who have experienced God's grace.

In his letter, Paul reminds the people of Corinth what they have witnessed, heard, and believed what God has done for them through the death and resurrection of Jesus Christ. Paul claims his identity in God's grace and reminds the Corinthians of the same.

Are you a list-maker? In camping ministry we are always preparing for guests and, therefore, always making lists of things to remember. Did we remember the food, the coffee, the toilet paper? Our intention behind all of the list-making is to help each person's experience of camp be one where they encounter Christ in a new way. We pray they may discover and experience Christ as they may need him: in forgiveness or in healing; in hopefulness or in new direction.

The message is clear and remains the same over time. Same God. Same resurrection. Same gift of grace. For Paul, the Corinthians, for us, and for all those we welcome. Paul reminded the Corinthians to listen and remember the message of those who have witnessed God's grace. How do you remember God's grace and love daily, and what does it mean for you this Lenten season, this day, this week?

As you continue through the journey of Lent, remember, as believers, we are called to be "proclaimers," those willing to give words to experiences that are part of our reality. We are resurrection people reminding ourselves, and others, of how God's grace is a reality and is available to each person. What is grace? In part it is both the God-given desire and power to experience, to understand, and to do God's will to our fullest. Read the passages for today. Let them fill you and remind you of what God has done for you, and how he desires to use you. It is far more than you imagine; go for it!

God of creation, thank you for the gift of your grace and amazing love poured out to us through the death and resurrection of Jesus Christ. Give us eyes to notice your Spirit in our lives and moving in our world, reminding us of your love. May we not be afraid to proclaim your love to those around us. During these days of the season of Lent, keep reminding us of all you do for us through Jesus, alive in us.

Andrea Scofield serves as the executive director of Camp Lutherwood Oregon, a year-round camp and retreat ministry in the coastal foothills of Oregon.

Thursday of Eastertide

CAMERON ANDERSON

❖

*While they were talking and discussing, Jesus himself came near
and went with them . . .*
Luke 24:15

*Moses did not know that the skin of his face shone because he had
been talking with God.*
Exodus 34:29b

Guess Who's Coming to Dinner?

Deep in conversation, Cleopas and his companion traveled on foot from Jerusalem to Emmaus—a seven-mile walk. There was much to discuss. Women arriving at the tomb where Jesus had been buried reported that his body was missing. Moreover, these same visitors claimed they had "seen a vision of angels who reported that he was alive" (Luke 24:23). Still, the two travelers were overcome by sadness because Jesus—the One who came to them as "a prophet mighty in deed and word" (Luke 24:19)—had been crucified. So far as they knew, Israel's Redeemer was gone.

As they walked on side by side, Luke's gospel tells us that Jesus joined them, but "their eyes were kept from recognizing him" (Luke 24:16). For readers, the anticipation builds. "Hey," we want to shout, "Jesus is right there with you!" Beginning with Moses, the master teacher recounted the whole salvation story to them. His identity, however, remained opaque.

Since the three travelers arrived at Emmaus near nightfall, Cleopas and his friend invited Jesus to stay with them for a meal. Face to face around the table as Jesus "took bread, blessed and broke it, and gave it to them" (Luke 24:30) their eyes were opened. Jesus had been with them all along.

Following this startling revelation, two surprising things happen: suddenly, Jesus vanishes from their sight and, within the hour, Cleopas and his companion rush back to Jerusalem (walking, this time, through the dark night) to announce to Jesus' disciples and friends that they have seen the resurrected Christ. At the close of this Lenten season and alongside Cleopas and his companion, we celebrate the fact that death could not hold the Son of Man.

But there is yet one more thing to learn. Observe that three or four short days after his death, Jesus was back at work teaching, guiding, and leading. Yes, his work on the cross was finished. Sin and death had been conquered. But the business of making disciples carries on. Thanks be to God. As we journey through life's sorrows, joys, trials, and wonders, the resurrected Christ continues to open our eyes. He is present with us.

We thank you God that, according to your mercy, you remain present with us in the world. May our hearts be warmed as, by your Word and your Spirit, you teach us. Keep us until that day when, like Cleopas and his friend, we meet you face to face.

Cameron Anderson is an artist and writer. He and his wife, Cynthia, live with Séamus, their cocker spaniel, in Madison, Wisconsin.

Friday of Eastertide

THOMAS KRISE

❖

JOHN 20:1–23 • EPHESIANS 4:17–32

When you talk, do not say harmful things, but say what people
need—words that will help others become stronger. Then what you
say will do good to those who listen to you.
Ephesians 4:29 (NCV)

Becoming Bridge Builders

As Jesus' resurrection gives Christians new life, this verse
reminds us that our words represent that new life. All of us have
had teachers who built us up with their words or who destroyed
our confidence with different words. My tenth-grade English
teacher, Mrs. Bonita Aiken, was one of the first to give me the
idea that I might be good at writing. Her support impressed upon
me the power others can have—for good or ill—just by a word.

As a teacher, Jesus knew that we are often obligated by faith
to say words that many don't want to hear. Words of challenge,
words of confrontation, words of discipline. Some words are no
fun to hear, but necessary for our becoming who we are created to
be. Those words must be said, but we must say them in ways that
"help others become stronger" (Eph. 4:29 NCV). At my university,
we've engaged in a series of "Race Chats" for faculty, staff, and
students that focus on "stories, not solutions." All in attendance

tell stories about being on the outside of a group, on the inside of a group, of helping an outsider become an insider, etc. In this way, we learn about issues of racial justice through words and in contexts that help us seek solutions that might work. In our university community, we try and live out the power of Jesus' resurrection through our words.

We have seen how this deepens friendships, sharpens understanding, builds trust and bridges, and moves us to a place where people can thrive and grow. The words become the Spirit at work in our midst.

Dear Lord, help us to speak words that build one another up and make people stronger. Help us use our teaching moments to build up the lives of our families, our work and our nation. Amen.

Thomas Krise is the president of Pacific Lutheran University. He and his wife, Patricia Love Krise, live in Tacoma, Washington.

Saturday of Eastertide

SHAILA VISSER

❊

JOHN 20:24–30 • JOHN 21:1–23

Jesus said to him, "Have you believed because you have seen me?
Blessed are those who have not seen and yet have come to believe."
John 20:29

Another Step Closer

Believing and unbelieving are dynamic, not static; alive, not just ideals. We are always moving in one direction or another, growing or sliding, getting stronger or plateauing. Things were not going well for Thomas: too many confusing things were happening; he was moving away and doubting Jesus. In this passage, Jesus shows up in a new and surprising way and he extends his love to Thomas by revealing himself. Jesus calls him to stop doubting and experience Christ in a new, unexpected, and more real way.

During this season of Lent we are called again in this passage to believe; to take another step toward Christ, allowing his Spirit to call us into deeper places of trust. But how do we lay aside our doubts? By turning again to Christ and surrendering of our incomplete and shaky unbelief, leaning in again to the work of the Holy Spirit in our lives to build our faith. The weight of unbelief is like a drag on our walk with Christ, and we need to daily cry out "Come, Holy Spirit, and change me." Will you let him? Will you take a step of faith again today to proclaim, "My Lord and my God?" Will our doubts define us? Will our questions become the self-protective tools to dodge dealing with the new realities of the experience of Christ that is beyond our understanding?

Peter describes such believers: "Although you have not seen him, you love him; and even though you do not see him now, you believe in him and rejoice with an indescribable and glorious joy, for you are receiving the outcome of your faith, the salvation of your souls" (1 Peter 1:8–9). We discover that Christ invites us to give as much of ourselves as we understand, to as much of him as we understand, and keep on doing that our whole lives! We realize there is no place to just settle in, park, or stop growing. He is beyond our understanding but eager to make himself fully known. Dare we respond, risk, and . . . live?

> *Father God, would you please grow in me a*
> *deeper level of trust in you? Please move by*
> *your Spirit to root out the unbelief and fill it*
> *with faith in you. Come, Holy Spirit. Amen.*

Shaila Visser is the national director of Alpha Canada. Shaila and her husband, Ryan, have been married for seventeen years, and live in Vancouver, British Columbia, Canada.

The Ripple

Where the ripple goes,
no one can fully know.
Sometimes the wave
gently washes over with only a whisper.
Other times the motion dislodges even that which
seemed so firm.

The choice, the whim, the urge,
the hope, the fear, the move so slight and small.
What brings the ripple?
It's often hard to know.

A rock thrown from a distant shore,
a presence in the pond seeking release,
The food chain moving thru its ways,
Or some unknown thing we hope to know.

Our lives do ripple and then recede.
Though often unaware, we hope
for good and cast our lives
to things and those we love
and pray the ripple grows and goes.

NOTES

The Supper at Emmaus
by Matthias Stom (c. 1600–c. 1652)

Matthias Stom was a Dutch painter who practiced his art in Italy (Naples and Sicily). He was significantly influenced by the Dutch artists who sought to emulate the style and techniques of the Italian artistic innovator, Caravaggio, such as was Dirck van Baburen (see Week 1 painting), those referred to as the "Utrecht *Caravaggisti.*"[18]

To notice: (1) The text portrayed here is Luke 24:30–31: "And it happened that, while he was with them at table, he took bread, said the blessing, broke it, and gave it to them. With that their eyes were opened and they recognized him, but he vanished from their sight" (NABRE). Stom is capturing the last second before Jesus would "vanish," because he is still blessing the bread and has not yet given it them. (2) Consider that for him "to vanish" means that they are given the capacity not to look *at* him, but with their eyes bright with understanding to look *toward that about which* he has been teaching them . . . such that they do not notice him—the greatest moment for a true Teacher. (3) The two disciples are talking too much, as is often the case with us humans, and so they are still arguing and justifying themselves and being clever with Jesus when Jesus has become still and is about to replay for them the beginning of the Passion at the Last Supper.

Scala / Art Resource, NY

Notes

1. Leonard J. Slatkes, "Baburen, Dirck van," *Grove Art Online*, *Oxford Art Online*, Oxford University Press, http://www.oxfordartonline.com/subscriber/article/grove/art/T005524.

2. Ann Weems, *Psalms of Lament* (Louisville, KY: John Knox Press, 1995), 67.

3. Jim Dodson, ThePilot.com, "Treasured Definition of Life," February 14.

4. Nina Mallory, "Greco, El," *The Oxford Companion to Western Art*, *Oxford Art Online*, Oxford University Press, http://www.oxfordartonline.com/subscriber/article/opr/t118/e1113.

5. Sin turns us in on ourselves as St. Augustine captured in his phrase *homo incurvatus in se* ("a person curved in on himself or herself").

6. A. W. Tozer, *Who Put Jesus on the Cross?* (Camp Hill, PA: WingSpread, 2009), e-book. Quoted in Alcorn, Randy (2015-09-17). *Happiness* (p. 452). Tyndale House Publishers, Inc. Kindle Edition.

7. Phillips Brooks and Lewis H. Redner, "O Little Town of Bethelem," 1868.

8. Michael Jaffé, "Dyck, Anthony van," *Grove Art Online*, *Oxford Art Online*, Oxford University Press, http://www.oxfordartonline.com/subscriber/article/grove/art/T024345.

9. Source unknown.

10. Thomas Nichols, "Tintoretto," *Grove Art Online*, *Oxford Art Online*, Oxford University Press, http://www.oxfordartonline.com/subscriber/article/grove/art/T085169pg1.

11. Emily Dickinson, "Tell All the Truth but Tell It Slant" from *The Poems of Emily Dickinson: Reading Edition*, ed. by Ralph W. Franklin. Copyright © 1998 by Emily Dickinson. Reprinted by permission of The Belknap Press of Harvard University Press.

12. The *Oxford English Dictionary* Online defines "intractable": "Not to be guided; not manageable or docile; uncontrollable; refractory, stubborn."

13. The Fourfold Franciscan Blessing; *The Way of the Cross* Women of the Gospels; Liturgy Training Publications Out of print.

14. Hans Vlieghe, "Rubens, Peter Paul," *Grove Art Online, Oxford Art Online*, Oxford University Press, http://www.oxford artonline.com/subscriber/article/grove/art/T074324.

15. http://www.wholesomewords.org/echoes/moody.html.

16. https://trustingortripping.wordpress.com/2013/07/26/this -is-the-end-but-for-me-it-is-the-beginning-of-life/

17. J. R. R. Tolkien, *The Return of the King*, kindle edition (Houghton Mifflin Harcourt), 270.

18. Leonard J. Slatkes, "Stom, Matthias," *Grove Art Online, Oxford Art Online*, Oxford University Press, http://www. oxfordartonline.com/subscriber/article/grove/art/T081526

MJM Grantees

4word • Abuse Recovery Ministry and Services • Acton Institute for the Study of Religion and Liberty • Adventist World Aviation • Africa New Life Ministries International • Aglow International • Argos International • Alaska Christian College • Alaska Pacific University • Aldersgate Conference Center • All God's Children International • Alliance Defending Freedom • Alpha Ministries Canada • Alpha North America • Amerson Music Ministries • Anchorage Christian Schools • Arctic Barnabas • Arctic Broadcasting • Arrow Leadership • Association of Christian Schools International • Association of Gospel Rescue Missions • Bakke Graduate University • Barnabas Family Ministries • Beartooth Mountain Christian Ministries • Beartooth Mountain Christian Ranch • Bend Area Habitat for Humanity • BeUndivided • Bible Mennonite Fellowship • Big Table • Biola University, Inc. • Birch Community Services, Inc. • Black Lake Bible Camp • Blanchet Catholic School • Blessed Earth, Inc. • Blood:Water Mission, Inc. • Blue Mts Conservative Baptist Assoc. • Boise Rescue Mission • Breakthrough Partners • Bridge Builders International • BridgeTown, Inc. • Brother Francis Shelter Kodiak • C3 Leaders • Calvary's Northern Lights Mission • Calvin College • Camp Bethel • Camp Bighorn • Camp Lutherwood • Camp Qwanoes • Camp Spalding • Camp Tapawingo • Campus Crusade for Christ, Inc. • Canadian Inter-Varsity Christian Fellowship • Cannon Beach Conference Center • Capitol Ministries • Care Net • Care Net Pregnancy and Family Services of Puget Sound • Carroll College • Cascades Camp • Catholic Broadcasting Northwest • Catholic Charities • Catholic Social Services Center • Cedar Springs Camp • Center for Religious Humanism • Center for Transforming Mission • Central Catholic High School • China Outreach Ministries, Inc. • Christ Clinic • Christian Camp and Conference Association International • Christian College Coalition • Christian International Scholarship Foundation • Christian Media Ministries • Christian Schools International • Christianity Today International • Church Initiative • Clydehurst Christian Ranch • Coffee Oasis • College of Idaho • Columbia Adventist Academy • Community Leadership and Development, Inc. • Community Leadership Development • Community Pregnancy Clinic • Compass Center • Compassion Connect, Inc. • Concordia University • Congregations for the Homeless • Conservative Baptist Foreign Mission Society and World Venture • Corban University • Cornerstone Christian Academy for Learning and Leadership • Council for Christian Colleges & Universities • Covenant Bible Camp • Covenant House Alaska • Crisis Pregnancy Centers • CRISTA Ministries • Cup of Cool Water • De La Salle North Catholic High School • Dinner & A Movie • Eagle Wings Ministries • Earl Palmer Ministries • East West Ministries International • Eastern Oregon Mission • Eastside Corps of the Salvation Army, Northwest Division, Western Territory • East-West Ministries International • Ecumenical Ministries of Oregon • Eugene Bible College • Faithful Friends • Family Renewal Shelter • Fellowship Foundation • Fellowship of Christian Athletes • Fir Point Bible Camp • Firm Foundation School • Firs Bible and Missionary Conference • Flathead Lutheran Bible Camp • Flying H Youth Ranch • Flying Mission USA • Focus on the Family • Forward Edge International • Foundation for Healthy Relationships • Friends of Menucha • Friends of the Family Ministries • Friendship House • Fruitland Bible Camp • Full Circle Exchange International, Inc. • Fuller Theological Seminary • Genesis Institute • George Fox University • Girl Scouts • Global Generosity Movement, Inc. • Gonzaga University • Gordon College • Gospel Missionary Union • Grace Christian School • Great Falls Rescue Mission • Greater Missoula Youth for Christ, Inc. • Habitat for Humanity • Habitat for Humanity of Snohomish County • Haller Lake Christian Health Clinic • Helping Hands • Holden Village, Inc. • Holy Name School • HOPE Center Moscow, Inc. • Hope in Christ Ministries • HopeCentral • Housing Hope • Immaculate Conception School • Immaculate Heart Retreat Center • INN University Ministries • Intermountain Deaconess Children's Services • International Christian Communications • International Justice Mission • International Students, Inc. • InterVarsity Christian Fellowship – USA • Jesuit High School • Jesuit Volunteer Corps • John Jay Institute for Faith, Society, and Law, Inc. • Jonah Ministries • Jubilee Reach • Kennedy Catholic High School • Kittitas County Chaplaincy • Klamath Falls Gospel Mission • KLEOS Ministries • KNOM Radio Mission, Inc. • Kodiak Baptist Mission • Krista Foundation for Global Citizenship • Leadership Catalyst • Leadership Development Seminars • Life Services • Life Way Pregnancy Services, Inc. dba Echoz Pregnancy Care Center • Light Side • Lighthouse Christian Ministries • Lighthouse of God Mission, Inc. • LINC Ministries • Living Water International • Luis Palau Association • Lutheran Community Services Northwest • Lutheran Family Services • Lutheran Outdoor Ministries • Lutherhaven Ministries, Inc. • MarriageTeam • Medical Teams International • Mending the Soul Ministries • Mending Wings • Mercy Corps • Mike Silva Evangelism • Military Community Youth Ministries • Ministry Coaching International • Mission Aviation Fellowship • Missoula 3:16 • Montana Bible College • Montana Rescue Mission • Moody Bible Institute of Chicago • Mountain View Community Center • Multnomah University • My Father's House • National Christian Charitable Foundation, Inc. • Navigators • Nehemiah Ministries • New Earth/Tierra Nueva • New Hope Farms • New Horizons Ministries • New Tribes Mission • Newberg Area Habitat for Humanity • North Park University • Northern Light Network • Northwest Baptist Seminary • Northwest Christian College • Northwest Family Services • Northwest Leadership Foundation • Northwest Nazarene University • Northwest University • Open Arms International • Open House • Operation Nightwatch • Opportunity International, Inc. • Oregon Episcopal School • Oregon Leadership Development Institute • Our Lady of Lourdes School • Our Lady of the Rosary • Pacific Association for Theological Studies • Pacific Lutheran University • Parachute Ministries • Partners International • Peace Community

Center • Peacemaker Ministries • Peak 7 Adventures • Portland Adventist Community Services • Portland Christian Schools • Portland Leadership Foundation • Portland Lutheran School • Portland Rescue Mission • Portland Youth for Christ, Inc. • Poverello Center • Praxis, Inc. • Pregnancy Resource Centers • Prison Fellowship Ministries • Pro Athletes Outreach • Project PATCH • Puget Sound Christian Clinic • Q Place • Raphael House • Re:source Global • REACH • Reach Out & Care Wheels • Regent College • Reid Saunders Association • Relevate Group, Inc. • Rescue Missions of the Northwest • Rescue:Freedom International • Responder Life • Rock Mountain Bible Mission • Safe Place Ministries • Saint Martin's University • Salem Free Medical Clinic • Salem Leadership Foundation • Salvation Army in the Northwest • Sammamish Bible Camp Association and SAMBICA • ScholarLeaders International • Search Ministries • Seattle Association for Theological Education • Seattle Pacific University • Seattle School of Theology and Psychology • Seattle University • SEND International • Set Free Alaska, Inc. • Selton Catholic High School • Shepherd's House • Silver Lake Camp • Society of St. Vincent de Paul • SonBridge Community Center • Sonshine Bible Clubs • Special K Ranch, Inc. • Spokane Youth for Christ • St. Andrew Nativity School • St. Martin's College • St. Mary Catholic School • St. Mathew Parish • St. Pius X Catholic School • St. Stephen's Academy • St. Vincent de Paul • Stillwater Youth Center • Street Youth Ministries • Stronger Families • Sunnyside Counseling Center • Tacoma Rescue Mission • Tacoma-Pierce County Chaplaincy • Tape Ministries Northwest • Taproot Theatre • Teen Challenge International • The Grotto • The Navigators • The Seattle School for Psychology and Theology • These Numbers Have Faces • Tilikum Center for Retreats and Outdoor Ministries • To Shine Too • Transitional Youth • Tri-City Union Gospel Mission • Trinity Western University • Trout Creek Bible Camp, Inc. • Twin Rocks Friends Conference Association • Union Gospel Mission across the Northwest • United Indian Missions • University of Great Falls • University of Portland • Urban Impact • Valley Catholic Middle High School • Veritas Forum • Victory Ministries • Vine Maple Place • Vision House • Voice for Christ Ministries • Volunteers of America, Inc. dba VOA of Western Washington • Walla Walla University • Warm Beach Christian Camps • Warner Pacific College • WAY Media, Inc. • Wellspring Revival Ministries • West Hills Christian School • West Sound Youth for Christ, Inc. • Western Conservative Baptist Seminary • Western Seminary • Westgate Baptist Church • Westside Christian High School • Whitworth University • Wiconi International • Wild Canyon Events • Wilderness Trails, Inc. • Windrider Institute • Wings of Hope • World Vision • Wycliffe Bible Translators • Yellowstone Baptist College • Yellowstone Boys and Girls Ranch • YMCA of the Northwest • Young Life • Young Life of Canada • You're Not Alone • Youth Dynamics • Youth for Christ • Youth Transition Network

Four Quartets

The dove descending breaks the air
With flame of incandescent terror
Of which the tongues declare
The one discharge from sin and error.
The only hope, or else despair
 Lies in the choice of pyre or pyre-
 To be redeemed from fire by fire.

Who then devised the torment? Love.
Love is the unfamiliar Name
Behind the hands that wove
The intolerable shirt of flame
Which human power cannot remove.
 We only live, only suspire
 Consumed by either fire or fire.
 —T. S. Eliot